BUYING AND SELLING A
BOOK *of* BUSINESS

BUYING AND SELLING A
BOOK *of* BUSINESS

*What Every Financial Advisor
and Planner Should Know*

Sandra E. Foster

HEADSPRING PUBLISHING
Toronto, Canada

Headspring Publishing
1370 Don Mills Road, Suite 300
Toronto, Ontario
M3B 3N7

National Library of Canada Cataloguing in Publication Data
Foster, Sandra E., 1955-
      Buying and selling a book of business: what every financial advisor and planner should know

IBSN 0-9689477-0-0

      1.   Business enterprises—Purchasing. 2. Sale of business enterprises. 3. Financial advisors—Marketing. 4. Investment advisors—Marketing. I. Title.

HG179.5.F68 2001   332.6'068'1   C2001-903042-8

Production Credits
Cover design: David Cobban
Text design: Wendy McLean
Printer: Transcontinental Printing
Cover Photo: Digital Vision Photography

Printed in Canada

CONTENTS

Preface   x

Chapter 1. Introduction   **1**
Who's Buying In Today's Marketplace?   1
   Strategic Buyers   1
   Marketing Buyers   2
Valuations   2
12 Steps To Buying Or Selling A Practice   4
   Step 1: Self-Assessment   5
   Step 2: Finding The Other Party   5
   Step 3: Preliminary Discussions Between Buyer And Seller   7
         Sample Non-Disclosure Agreement   8
   Step 4: Performing The First Level Of Due Diligence   8
   Step 5: Assessing The Opportunity   9
   Step 6: Preparing The Letter Of Intent With Initial Deposit   10
   Step 7: Further Due Diligence To Assess The Practice   11
   Step 8: Arranging For Financing   12
   Step 9: Making A Formal Offer   12
   Step 10: Negotiating And Making A Counter-Offer   13
   Step 11: Signing Other Agreements Related To The
         Transaction   13
   Step 12: Implementing The Transition Plan   14

Chapter 2. For Buyers and Potential Buyers Only   **15**
Advantages To Buying An Existing Client Base   16
What Are You Buying?   17
Disadvantages To Buying An Existing Client Base   18
Buying Part Of A Book   19
Buying From An Advisor Who Is Retiring From The Business   20
What Does Your Ideal Business Look Like?   21
How Much Risk Are You Prepared To Take On?   22
Summary   23

Chapter 3. For Sellers and Potential Sellers Only   **25**
Is It Yours To Sell?   25
Why Do You Want To Sell?   28
What Are You Selling?   29
What Are You Looking For In A Buyer?   30
Preparing Your Business For Sale   31
   Increase Your Revenues   32
   Run A More Efficient Practice   33
   Build Deep, Loyal Client Relationships   33
   Watch Your Product Mix   35
Auditing Your Practice   35
   Profile Your Practice   35
   Make Sure Your Housekeeping Is Up-To-Date 36
   What Else Do You Want From The Deal?   37
Summary   37

Chapter 4. Methods of Valuing a Practice   **39**
The Five Most Common Valuation Methods   40
Assets Under Management   43
Historical Commission And Fee Income   44
Historical Annual Recurring Revenues   46
Revenues Actually Received   47
   Income And Revenues Before Or After The Grid? 49
Free Cash Flow   50
   Reviewing The Seller's Financial Statements 52
Summary   54

Chapter 5. Factoring Attrition Into the Equation   **57**
What Is A Good Retention Rate?   58
How To Reduce Client Attrition   59
Some Ways To Factor Attrition Into The Purchase Price   60
Summary   61

**Chapter 6. Factors That Increase/Decrease the
      Purchase Price**   **63**
General Factors   64
Revenues And Profitability   65
   Concentration   66
   Commission Versus Fee Income   66
   Other Sources Of Revenue   66
   Revenue And Profit Pattern   67
   Direction Of Fees And Payouts   67
Client Assets   67
   Poor Investment Decisions   68
   Assessing The Revenue Versus The Profitability Per Client 68
Client Base   70
   Client Loyalty   71
   Elderly Client Base   71

Potential Synergies 71
More Questions For Every Potential Buyer To Consider 72
Summary 73

Chapter 7. Show Me the Money! Paying For the Business **75**
Key Financing Factors 76
Sample Promissory Note 77
Vendor-take-back Financing 77
Size Of The Down Payment 78
Risk Of Default 79
The Traditional Lender 79
Your Firm 80
Stock Or Stock Options 80
Summary 81

Chapter 8. Finalizing the Deal **83**
Negotiating The Terms Of The Deal 83
The Seller's Staff 84
The Prospect List 84
Bringing In New Clients 85
Transfer Fees 85
Minimizing The Tax 85
Commissioned Employees 86
Incorporated Advisors and Planners 86
Other Taxes 87
Work In Progress 87
Calling In The Professionals 88
The Paperwork 89
Non-Compete Agreement 89
Sample Non-Compete Covenant 90
Purchase And Sale Agreement 91
The Terms And Conditions Of The Offer 93
The Client Assets 93
Adjustments Or Bonuses 93
Other Assets 94
The Transition Plan 94
Role Of Seller During Transition Period 94
Transition Salaries And Expenses 94
When To Close 94
Warranties And Guarantee Of Each Party 95
Extent Of Liability 95
Dispute Resolution 95
Management Consulting Contracts Or Service Agreements 96
Summary 96

Chapter 9. The Transition Plan **97**
The Introductions 98
Introduce The Buyer To The Seller's Clients 98

Introduce The Clients To The Buyer's Staff   100
Introduce The Buyer To The Seller's Centre Of Influences   101
Introduce The Transaction To The Buyer's Existing Clients   101
The Client Meetings   101
    One-On-One Meetings With Clients   101
    How Many Meetings Will You Have?   103
The Administration   103
    Complete The Paperwork To Transfer The Client Accounts   103
        Client Paperwork   103
        Block Transfers   104
    Train The Buyer And Their Staff On Procedures And Systems   104
    Seller To Provide Buyer With Sample Form Letters,
        Newsletters, Statements And Reports Used   104
    Seller To Provide Buyer With Client Word Processing
        And Spreadsheet Files   105
    Make Sure All Accounts Transfer To The Buyer   105
    Seller's Housekeeping   105
Summary   105

Chapter 10. Keys to Success   **107**

Appendices   **113**
A. Sample Purchase And Sale Agreement   113
B. Worksheets To Profile The Practice   119
    Income And Revenue Details   121
    Expenses   125
    Client Assets   128
    Profile Of Clients   133
    Profiling The Advisor And The Practice   136
    Other Assets For Sale   142

Interested In Buying or Selling a Book Of Business?   **145**
Confidential Registry   145
Consulting Services For Buyers And Sellers   145

About Headspring Consulting Inc.   **147**

About Sandra Foster   **149**

PREFACE

The buying and selling of financial advisory practices is a relatively new transaction. In 1993, one broker told me that he "sold" his book with $35 million in assets under administration for $12,000. In the late 90s, some advisors were negotiating deals for one times gross revenue, and even higher valuations. But by 2001, many financial advisors and planners had become more interested in practices that had real profits, not just assets under management.

By the time I sold my practice in 1999, I had spent months researching the valuation of businesses and professional service practices in general, and especially financial advisory and planning practices in the U.S. and Canada.

Since then, I have been invited to give presentations and workshops from coast to coast on buying and selling a book of business and how to create an effective succession plan. I've also been asked by numerous sellers to help them prepare their business for sale to maximize the value of their business, and by buyers to help them assess the practice they are considering buying. As well, I've been asked by firms to help them establish internal guidelines to facilitate succession planning among their financial advisors and planners.

This book examines the buying and selling of financial advisory and planning practices; from finding an interested buyer or seller, negotiating the purchase price, integrating clients into an existing client base, developing strong bonds with those clients, and other ideas everyone involved in the transaction — buyers, sellers and their professional advisors — should consider.

This book considers both sides of the transaction. The better you understand the "sell" side and the "buy" side, the better equipped you will be to enter into a successful transaction, regardless of whether you are a buyer or a seller.

Even if you're not planning to buy or sell in the near future, understanding the factors and issues that go into valuing a business can help you maximize the current value and profitability of your own business — and its future value. As well, understanding the methods of valuing a practice is becoming an issue in wrongful dismissal cases, as well as for planners and advisors who are separating or divorcing their spouse.

If you're selling, this book will help you:

- clarify what you hope to find in a buyer
- negotiate a fair price and favourable terms
- ensure the well-being of your clients
- manage the transition period.

The bad news is that your practice may not be worth as much as you think. The good news is that by taking the right steps, sellers should be able to increase the value of their business. Understanding the methods for determining the value of a business and the soft issues involved in the transaction can help you ensure the purchase price is fair. At some firms, clients and their assets are considered to be owned by the firm, not the advisor — these advisors are not allowed to sell their practice.

If you're buying, this book will help you:

- avoid paying too high a price
- negotiate favourable financing terms
- maximize client retention
- walk away from the wrong deal.

Buying an existing book of clients from another advisor can instantly increase the assets the advisor has, take the business to the next production level, or jump-start a newer business.

Throughout the book, I will be referring to financial planners, advisors and consultants as financial advisors. I will also be using the terms "financial advisory practice," "financial planning practice" and "the business" interchangeably.

Let the negotiations begin!

Words of Caution

The material contained in this book is for educational purposes only and represents the opinion of the author. Care has been taken to ensure the accuracy of the information contained in this book at the time it was published. Readers should be aware that there is currently no standard method for valuing a financial advisory or planning practice and this material and its references reflect practices that are subject to change.

This book contains information of a general nature to help you understand the general issues related to buying or selling a financial advisory or planning practice. You will find examples, tools, checklists and worksheets to help you assess the key points for planning and negotiating the deal. The names used are fictious and any resemblance to anyone is purely coincidental.

This book is not designed as a do-it-yourself guide and it does not exhaust all the considerations or provide solutions for every situation. Sample documents are included to help you understand the agreements discussed in this book. They should not be used to prepare your own legal paperwork. It is sold with the understanding that the information that follows is not a substitute for consulting a professional who can apply the most current practices and specialized legal and tax advice to your particular situation. There is no guarantee that this book contains everything you need to know. Readers are encouraged to obtain professional legal, tax and financial advice on how these ideas might fit their own situation before deciding on a course of action.

Although this material has been carefully researched and prepared, the publisher and Sandra Foster do not accept any legal responsibility for its contents or for any consequences arising from its use.

➊ INTRODUCTION

*"It isn't what you make...
it's what you do with what you make."*
Ralph A. Hayward

Whether you are looking at growing your practice or considering how long you will stay in the business, buying or selling a financial advisory or planning practice is a topic you'll ultimately face.

Creating value in your business affects every aspect of your practice—from the way you work with clients, your systems and its day-to-day operations to the products you sell and the firm you work for. While you are active in the business, you can profit today by increasing its value—and may be able to profit from its sale value when it is time to exit the business.

WHO'S BUYING IN TODAY'S MARKETPLACE?

There are basically two types of buyers of financial advisory and planning practices in the marketplace, strategic buyers and marketing buyers.

Strategic Buyers

To make things simplistic (almost to the point of error), a strategic buyer tends to be a corporate buyer who is interested in acquiring blocks of business and/or a larger distribution network. A deal with a strategic buyer may include:

- a purchase price as well as an equity stake in the acquiring firm
- succession terms for the eventual retirement of the seller
- buyout on the death of the seller
- restrictive clauses the seller must agree to.

The seller may also be required to commit to working for the strategic buyer for a period of time and/or to meet some performance targets. The "seller" is not selling his or her business up front—but they may be agreeing to sell their business to the acquiring firm in the future. Selling to a strategic buyer does not normally offer a quick exit.

Marketing Buyers

Marketing buyers tend to be individual financial advisors or planners who are looking to acquire an established client base to expand their business and complement their other marketing programs such as seminars, advertising and referrals. In fact, buying a practice and having the seller refer their client base may be the ultimate (certainly the largest) referral! This book focuses on the purchase and sale of financial advisory and planning practices between marketing buyers and sellers who want to leave the business.

VALUATIONS

When I offer workshops on buying or selling a book of business, I often profile a practice and ask half of the audience to role-play being a seller and set a price for that practice. Then I ask the other half to role-play being a potential buyer and determine what they would be willing to pay for it. Regardless of the practice profiled, sellers either grossly over-estimate or under-estimate its value, and at least one person in the audience wants $500,000 firm. The prices buyers would pay are

Here are just some of the formulas that have been used to value financial advisory and planning practices.

1. 40 bps of AUM based on assets at the time of sale, with seller's assistance during the transition limited to one month. 50 percent of the purchase price paid as a down payment with the balance paid in full 6 months later.

2. 50 bps of AUM paid up-front based on assets at time of sale. Seller moved into management position at firm and provided ongoing transition and mentoring support over a 12-month period. Another 50 bps paid one year later based on assets at that time.

3. 1.5 x historical annual recurring revenue equal to 18 months of trailer fees as of the transaction date paid in quarterly instalments over 18 months, no deposit. Advisor left industry and provided limited support during transition.

4. Book of GIC business sold for 1.5 times the total gross revenue earned in the last 12 months.

5. Between two advisors with the same firm, one advisor bought the other's smaller clients. Future gross commissions were to be split with 80 percent to the seller, 20 percent to the buyer for 2½ years using a joint dealer/rep code. Selling advisor provides limited transition support.

6. Advisor sold his clients to an advisor at a different firm for 2 times net historical recurring revenues, with 20 percent held back for attrition. Only if retention of assets was 80 percent or better would the buyer pay the seller the remaining 20 percent.

7. One-time annual historical commissions and fee income, with 50 percent paid up-front, and the other half paid semi-annually over 24 months.

8. Up-front purchase price based on 60 bps of AUM. If 90 percent retention achieved after 18 months, bonus of 25 bps of AUM on assets retained.

9. Three times the historical recurring revenues, after the production grid, paid as follows: one-third down, one-third over four quarters and balance at 18 months.

10. One times the historical annual income, after the grid, with nothing down. 90 percent of purchase price paid over 12 months. Balance paid out at 12 months only if retention target of 90 percent were achieved.

Throughout the book, we'll discuss various methods for setting a purchase price.

clustered — they all seem to be using some method to come up with a value.

In 1999 and early 2000, the stock market was hot and there were more interested buyers than sellers. The bidding wars had started for financial advisory and planning practices. Some buyers were anticipating continued growth and with the corresponding potential for profits, were willing to pay premium prices. Maybe Nortel Networks wasn't the only business priced for perfection. In mid-2001, the stock market continued to slump and clients and prospects were sitting on the fence with their money. Falling revenues were negatively impacting the potential purchase price for a practice. There were still more interested buyers than sellers. Few were willing to sell for less than they might have realized just months earlier.

While "assets under management" (AUM) is one of the markers the financial services industry uses to determine whether or not their advisor is successful, it can be a mistake to use it to determine a purchase price for a practice because it does not consider the quality of the client assets or the profitability of the advisor's practice. Today's buyers are looking for profitable practices, not just assets under management.

12 STEPS TO BUYING OR SELLING A PRACTICE

There are 12 steps involved in buying or selling a financial advisory or planning practice.

Some of the steps will be done sequentially; others happen simultaneously. If the practice is very small, some of the steps might be combined. Every transaction goes through all or most of the following steps, which include:
1. Self-assessment
2. Finding the other party
3. Preliminary discussions
4. Performing the first level of due diligence
5. Assessing the opportunity

6. Preparing the letter of intent, with initial deposit
7. Further due diligence to assess the value of the practice
8. Arrange for financing
9. Making the formal offer
10. Negotiating and making a counter-offer
11. Signing other agreements related to the transaction
12. Developing a transition plan.

Step 1. Self-Assessment

Every potential buyer and seller needs to do their own self-assessment to determine what they are looking for and why they are interested in buying or selling a practice. Knowing where you are today and where you want to go are part of this self-assessment. Have you taken the steps to maximize the value of your practice and the loyalty of your clients? Have you prepared a succession plan? Have you done your own personal financial plan? It's ironic that many financial advisors and planners work hard with clients to help them achieve financial independence and their life goals, yet have not taken the time to do planning for themselves.

When you know what you are looking for and your bottom line will help identify the right opportunity and enable you to quickly pass on the wrong opportunity, saving you time (and time is money).

You'll find self-assessment tools in the chapters titled For Buyers Only and For Sellers Only.

Step 2. Finding The Other Party

Finding the other party to your potential transaction is an important step. If you are looking to sell, it may be hard to match up with a qualified potential buyer even though they may be looking for you. It's generally not well accepted to say you are looking to leave the business, and to date, most completed deals have been relatively low-key transactions.

Sellers may also want to keep their intentions private to protect their business and their clients from competitors, and in doing so, may inadvertently limit the likelihood of multiple offers and their final price. However, at the time of writing, my surveys tell me that the number of interested buyers outnumbers interested sellers by a margin of about 10 to 1, making it a seller's market. But as the industry changes and advisors age, the number of people interested in selling their practice will increase.

Buyers and sellers find each other in different ways. The other party to your transaction could be a total stranger or someone you already know.

The key sources for finding a buyer or seller include:

- an advisor working at the same firm
- an advisor working at another firm
- word of mouth, advertising, a business broker or buy-and-sell registry
- a family member
- someone in a related field, such as an accountant
- a team member working for you who already knows the clients.

Don't overlook selling your practice to someone who is working for you. If you have a licensed assistant with the attributes to be a good advisor, they are already working with the clients and might have even more contact with them than you do. This could lead to enhanced client retention and enable you to exit the business gracefully.

TIP *While many advisors look at those reaching retirement age as potential sellers, it is not just experienced advisors who might want to sell. Some advisors with only a few years' experience may have some good clients, but not enough for them to earn a decent income.*

Step 3. Preliminary Discussions Between Buyer And Seller

It's important for the buyer and seller to meet face-to-face to size each other up and have a preliminary discussion regarding their respective businesses. Some transactions seem to stay in the preliminary discussion stage for years; but where the parties are very motivated, the transaction can move quickly to the next step.

Some sellers conduct this preliminary meeting somewhat like a job interview — an interview to select their successor. They assess the potential buyer's background and the skills they bring to the table by reviewing his or her resume and personal brochure. The potential buyer will also consider if the seller's perceived value of his or her business is reasonable and if there appears to be a good fit between the two practices, including the client base and approach to the business.

Where there appears to be a preliminary "meeting of the minds" and it seems worth discussing the opportunity in more detail, the potential seller will normally request that the potential buyer sign a non-disclosure agreement. Until this agreement is signed, the discussion may stay very preliminary and general.

TIP   *Include a clause that states when, or under what conditions the intentions of the buyer and the seller can be made public.*

A non-disclosure agreement helps to ensure that, should the transaction not go through, the buyer will not have the right to use any information revealed by the seller, such as the names of the clients. Sellers should not have to worry that a prospective buyer might be interested only in collecting the names of their clients to prospect to them directly, without consummating a sale. The agreement may also require the potential buyer not disclose any information to anyone, including the firm they work for, their staff or others, until authorized by the seller.

SAMPLE NON-DISCLOSURE AGREEMENT

Re: Tom Green at ABC Investments Inc.

I agree that any information disclosed to me by Tom Green of ABC Investments Inc. in connection with discussions regarding buying his book of clients will be considered proprietary and confidential, including all such information relating to Tom Green's past, present or future business activities, research, product design or development, trade secrets, personnel and business opportunities. Confidential information shall not include information previously known to me, the general public, or previously recognized as standard practice in the field.

I will not disclose our discussions to any person without written authorization. I acknowledge that unauthorized disclosure could cause irreparable harm and significant injury to Tom Green.

I shall not directly or indirectly, use, disseminate, disclose, communicate, divulge, reveal, publish, use for my own benefit, copy, make notes, input in a computer database, or preserve in any way any confidential information, unless I first receive written permission from an authorized Officer of the companies or their appropriate affiliates.

I will not make copies of such information and materials other than for my own use. I will take all steps necessary to preserve the confidentiality of any documents in my position, including and without limitation to their secure transportation, storage and handling.

Whether or not this transaction occurs, my obligation or confidentiality and non-use undertaken in this agreement shall survive indefinitely. I agree to return any documents or thing containing such information and/or materials immediately. I further agree that I shall not retain copies or notes.

Accepted and agreed to by:

Signature: _____

Name of Potential Purchaser

Step 4. Performing The First Level Of Due Diligence

Sellers eventually need to release information about their business to the potential buyer so they can conduct the first level of the due diligence process.

The buyer will want to see some of the business's confidential information, including revenue statements, assets summaries and production reports. They will want to understand the seller's method of doing business, the products they recommend and the procedures and systems they use. The buyer will also want to assess whether or not the business is being sold as an ongoing concern, and whether or not the seller will heartily endorse the new owner and assist during the transition period.

At this stage, the names of the clients are not generally revealed.

TIP *Sellers can use the Worksheets to Profile a Practice in the Appendix so they have the facts of their business to discuss with potential buyers when the time is right.*

Step 5. Assessing The Opportunity

The buyer will assess the opportunity, based on the discussions they have had with the seller and the reports and financial information that have been provided. They may also consult with a consultant or advisor experienced in the buying and selling of financial advisory and planning practices to determine an appropriate price range for the business.

See Chapter 6 titled Factors That Increase/Decrease The Purchase Price to help assess the business. Remember, the buyer is not going to find a practice that is a perfect fit with their own, but they are looking for a good fit.

IS THE BUSINESS A GOOD FIT?

A buyer not only has to consider the details of the business but whether or not the business will help them achieve their personal and professional goals.

Rate the opportunity on a scale of 1 to 10
(from 1=not at all to 10=absolutely)

This practice is an excellent match with my current clients	1 2 3 4 5 6 7 8 9 10
This practice is an excellent match with my ideal client	1 2 3 4 5 6 7 8 9 10
The clients have needs that are not being addressed	1 2 3 4 5 6 7 8 9 10
The price for the practice is fair and supportable	1 2 3 4 5 6 7 8 9 10
The practice will make excellent use of my education and expertise	1 2 3 4 5 6 7 8 9 10
I see ways to reduce the cost to service the clients	1 2 3 4 5 6 7 8 9 10
This practice is compatible with my mission statement	1 2 3 4 5 6 7 8 9 10

If you answered 7 or less for any of these questions, you need to carefully assess whether or not the practice has the potential to be a good fit over the long-term.

Step 6. Preparing The Letter Of Intent With Initial Deposit

If the potential buyer likes what they see and is interested in moving to the next stage, they will provide the potential seller with a letter of intent and an initial deposit. While not the same as a binding purchase and sale agreement (although the letter of intent may have some binding conditions), the letter of intent documents the discussions and the understanding of the transaction that have evolved between the buyer and seller up to this point, including:

- the preliminary purchase price or the formula or method to be used to establish the purchase price
- financing terms, particularly if the seller has indicated they would be willing to provide vendor-take-back financing
- how retention issues will be dealt with
- the seller's involvement during transition
- the proposed closing date
- preliminary undertakings by the buyer or the seller.

Since a significant amount of the seller's time may be involved in assisting with further due diligence work, the seller may require the buyer to provide an initial non-refundable deposit of $5,000 or five percent of the anticipated purchase price to indicate they are serious. The seller's lawyer would likely hold this deposit in trust.

TIP   *Sellers interested in getting the best possible price may not be willing to sign an agreement that would restrict them from soliciting an offer from another potential buyer.*

Step 7. Further Due Diligence To Assess The Practice

After the potential buyer has signed the letter of intent, they will conduct a deeper level of due diligence on the practice and on the financial and business records of the business. They will want to understand the practice and assess its sources of revenue and general financial condition, including any liabilities, to determine the ultimate purchase price they would be willing to pay.

The buyer will also want to audit the client details, including which clients generate the most revenue. The buyer will want to look at enough client files to determine that everything is complete and in order. Some buyers will assess each individual client before making the formal offer; others will spot-check the client files and include adjustment clauses in the purchase and sale agreement to deal with any client problems which might be discovered later.

While sellers will position their practice in the best possible light, they have the responsibility to advise the potential buyer of any material facts regarding their business. In fact, the buyer's lawyer will likely include a clause in the purchase and sale agreement whereby the seller warranties they have represented the business fairly and accurately.

The buyer might find some minor weaknesses in the seller's practice. These weaknesses normally do not affect the buyer's interest in the business, but they may affect the price the buyer offers. As well, the buyer will start to formulate what steps they might take during transition and beyond to address them.

If the potential buyer wants to buy the business, they will have their lawyer prepare the purchase and sale agreement to make a formal offer.

Step 8. Arrange For Financing

No deal is complete unless the buyer can raise the money to pay for the business, either through personal resources, traditional lender financing, assistance from their firm, or through vendor-take-back financing.

The initial offer to purchase may be conditional on the buyer being able to arrange financing or on the vendor taking back financing. Most buyers arrange any financing they require in advance so they can make an offer that is not conditional on financing.

Step 9. Making The Formal Offer

The purpose of the formal purchase and sale agreement is to document the terms of the agreement and provide the legal wording to protect both parties. While your letter of intent might be only three or four pages, the purchase and sale agreement could be 20 pages or more once all the legal clauses are added!

If the seller is extending vendor-take-back financing, this term will be included in the offer to purchase. This term can extend the relationship between the buyer and seller for years.

Step 10. Negotiating And Making A Counter-Offer

The terms of the initial offer to purchase drawn up by the buyer's lawyer may require modifications before they are acceptable to the seller. The agreement may go back and forth as counter-offers between the buyer and seller several times before all the terms are acceptable to both parties. The actual changes to the offer should become fewer and fewer with each revision.

Throughout the final negotiations, both the buyer and seller need to stay focused on what each is trying to accomplish. They should negotiate any points of contention, or sticky issues, as professionally as they can, and look for the appropriate compromises. Some find it helpful to bring in a mediator to maintain perspective and resolve issues.

TIP   *If the terms of the proposed deal seem to be unreasonable, or seem like they will become unreasonable, be prepared to walk away. Some of the worst deals are made when one of the parties feels pressured.*

Step 11. Signing Other Agreements Related To The Transaction

The transaction may involve other agreements between the buyer and seller, such as:
- a non-compete or non-solicitation agreement
- an agreement for the seller to provide ongoing management expertise
- ongoing service agreement
- an agreement to compensate the seller for any future leads they provide.

Some lawyers incorporate these as part of the purchase and sale agreement; others prepare separate agreements.

Step 12. Implementing The Transition Plan

The transition plan is crucial to the success of the buying and selling of a financial advisory or planning practice. The well-thought-out transition plan will contribute to better client retention and provide the buyer (and the clients) access to the "memory banks" of the selling advisor for a period of time.

How long the seller should stay involved with the clients and the business after transition is debatable. Some buyers invite the retiring advisor to future client events or are even willing to provide them with office space where they can "meet and greet" their old clients—as long as their conversations do not violate any securities rules and regulations. Other buyers feel the seller's prolonged presence would inadvertently interfere with their ability to develop relationships with the clients and prefer that the seller move on as soon as possible.

See the Chapter 9, titled The Transition Plan, for more details.

② FOR BUYERS AND POTENTIAL BUYERS ONLY

"Success won't just come to you.
It has to be met at least halfway."
Frank Tyger

There's no doubt about it. Buying a financial advisory or planning practice can double your client assets overnight! And double the amount of work for you and your team. But it may not double your revenues or your profits. You have to assess if you would be buying a business, or a book of business.

I've found that buyers tend to be overly optimistic about two key factors, one, the income they expect to make from the opportunity at hand, and two, the retention rate they expect — even before they've done any due diligence on the practice they are considering buying.

Purchasing a practice requires the buyer to make a number of commitments:
1. the financial commitment to pay the price
2. the professional commitment to provide advice and services to the clients and
3. a personal commitment to build a one-on-one relationship with each client.

ADVANTAGES TO BUYING AN EXISTING CLIENT BASE

Making the financial commitment to buy a business can be a fast way to gather assets and increase your revenues. And if your practice has excess capacity, such as time or staff, buying an existing business might let you take advantage of the resources you already have in place.

While buying an existing financial advisory or planning practice can be a strategic way to increase your assets and income; money is only part of the equation. A successful transaction also requires the buyer to invest sweat equity—their time and passion.

WHY BUY?

Why are you considering buying a financial advisory or planning practice? (Check all that apply)

❏ To increase my assets under administration because of my firm's recognition program

❏ To make more money

❏ To have the potential to make more money

❏ Jump-start my business

❏ To move to the next production level

❏ To utilize excess capacity to increase my profitability

❏ Grow my business faster than I could one client at a time

Before signing on the dotted line, every potential buyer should ask "could I build a better practice one client at a time for the same amount of money?" If the answer is "yes," the next question to consider is "how long would it take?" Even buying a business takes time, time to find the right practice to buy, time to assess that business and then the time spent with the new clients.

TIP   *Compare the cost of buying a business with what it would cost to grow your business one client at a time. Consider the capital you would need to invest, the amount of sweat equity it would require, and how long it would take.*

WHAT ARE YOU BUYING?

From the purely business perspective, you want to buy the revenue stream the business generates. In order to get that revenue stream, you acquire a list of clients and their assets, and an introduction to the seller's clients, but there is no guarantee that the seller's clients will become your clients. On the other hand, a well-thought-out transaction with a well-executed transition can have a high probability of success.

In addition to acquiring the seller's existing client assets, the buyer may also be acquiring:

- goodwill
- the seller's time during the transition period
- the seller's systems
- the reputation and brand of the company and its products and services
- prospect lists or databases
- company name
- office furniture and equipment
- computer hardware and software
- any real estate owned by the firm.

You may or may not be interested in the items that don't relate to the revenues generated by the clients and the seller's goodwill. You'll have to discuss with the prospective seller whether or not you would be required to purchase any of the non-client assets.

TIP   *Are you looking to buy a client base that has proven to be profitable? Or a client base that has the potential to be profitable? Or both?*

In this book, we will be focusing on the valuation of the client assets, revenues, profits and the seller's goodwill.

DISADVANTAGES OF BUYING AN EXISTING PRACTICE

While there can be advantages to buying an established client base, there are some potential disadvantages, including:

- It may be difficult to determine what you are buying. There might be issues lurking under the surface you don't see, or aren't aware of, until you actually sit down with the clients and ask them what they want from their advisor
- The transaction is usually an "all or none" transaction, where you buy all the clients and their assets, even the ones you don't really want to service
- There is a large volume of work to be done up front
- It's not easy for clients to change personal advisors
- There is no standard method for valuing a practice.

It's important to find a business that's a good fit, one that is similar to the business you are building. For example, if you want to deal with retirees, and you are given an opportunity to buy a practice full of young, high-tech computer types, you may not have a good fit. The challenge for all financial advisors—whether they have been in the business for a few months or many years—is to attract and retain profitable clients who value the services and advice they provide. If you commit to buying the wrong business and have to turn around and sell it to someone else, it is unlikely that you would be able to recoup your investment.

I've seen some proposed deals that would have been big business mistakes—where the buyers were focused on size of the client assets, rather than the types of clients and what would be required to service them.

There is no guarantee you will be able to find a suitable business to buy. Advisors should not abandon other methods of growing their business, such as through referrals, seminars and advertising.

BUYING PART OF A BOOK

A seller may want to streamline their practice and be offering only a portion of their client assets for sale. Perhaps they have a group of clients located in another town that they are having difficulty seeing, or are now focused in a tight niche market or a specific product line. Or perhaps they want to transfer some clients to someone more eager to serve them.

WHY ARE THEY SELLING?

If the seller is offering only part of their client assets, consider why.

Is it because they are:

❑ a drag on profitability?

❑ located in another part of the country?

❑ PITA (pain in the a__) clients?

❑ clients whose expectations are out of line?

❑ refocusing on a tight niche market?

❑ changing their business model, such as from commission to fee?

❑ refocusing on one product line?

❑ selling a client base that is too large for any one buyer, so they are selling to multiple buyers?

While some potential buyers are interested in a seller's top clients, most sellers offering only part of the business for sale are usually offering their smaller clients. Before buying an advisor's smaller clients, you should carefully examine the profitability of those client assets. I've heard it said that one-third of clients in the average advisor's book is profitable, one-third breaks even and the other third actually costs the advisor money to service them. If these clients are not profitable for the current advisor, you should carefully consider why you think they would be profitable for you.

TIP   *If you are considering buying the bottom one-third of a client's assets (the ones that are not profitable for the seller), what makes you think you can service them and turn a profit? If the answer is "not likely" you may be better off not acquiring them. Why would you want more work with no reward?*

BUYING FROM AN ADVISOR WHO IS RETIRING FROM THE BUSINESS

Acquiring the client assets from an advisor who is retiring from the business is the least complicated transaction, once they decide they are ready to leave. Selling a practice can be an emotional transaction for the retiring seller.

The selling advisor will likely have the time to assist in transitioning the client assets to the buyer — particularly if part of their final price depends on the success of the transition. On the other hand, if they have not thought-out their retirement, you could find them dropping by the office "just to see how things are going" after their services and expertise are no longer required.

If the selling advisor is selling part of their book or moving to another part of the financial services industry, the selling advisor may not have time to assist with the transition. This is not to say that these transitions cannot work, but both parties need to carefully plan what will be required.

TIP   *Keep in mind the types of clients who can benefit from the types of service and advice you provide. Some practices up for sale could create more headaches than benefits.*

WHAT DOES YOUR IDEAL BUSINESS LOOK LIKE?

Sometimes an opportunity to buy a business will come to a buyer. Be sure to take the time to reflect on the type of business you want to build. This will help you determine if the opportunity is worth pursuing.

Describe your ideal client

Stage of life _____

Time horizon _____

Investment philosophy _____

Investment objectives _____

Average client size _____

Practice focus

❑ Investment management

❑ Financial planning

❑ Integrated financial advice

Compensation

❑ Fees paid by client   ❑ Fees paid by product suppliers

❑ Commission   ❑ Combination

Annual Return on Investment (ROI), equal to return on

❑ Treasury bills   ❑ Large cap equity   ❑ Growth equity

❑ Venture capital   ❑ Other _____

Types of products

❑ Mutual Funds   ❑ Securities   ❑ Insurance

❑ Other _____

I want to:

❑ No   ❑ Yes   Create future sales

❑ No   ❑ Yes   Service existing clients

❑ No   ❑ Yes   Solve complex financial problems

❑ No   ❑ Yes   Manage a team of people

HOW MUCH BUSINESS RISK ARE YOU PREPARED TO TAKE ON?

When buying or selling any sort of business, there is risk. Some of the risks are the buyer's; some are the seller's. However, anything that affects the buyer's ability to complete the financial side of the transaction affects both parties.

> **TIP**   *If the asking price is based on overly optimistic assumptions, such as for market appreciation or client retention, the buyer risks paying too much.*

The level of risk inherent in the transaction (which is ultimately reflected in the purchase price) is determined by a number of factors, including:

- whether or not the buyer and the seller work at the same firm. The transaction with the least amount of risk is one where the buyer and the seller work at the same firm and deal with clients in a similar manner. The risk increases when the buyer and seller work at different firms. Not only will the clients have to accept a new advisor, they also have to transfer their assets to a new firm.
- the phase in the market cycle. If stock markets experience a major correction shortly after the business is sold, the buyer might not be able to earn enough to cover the instalments.
- the business continuing to operate the same as it has in the past. Downward pressures on production grids, fees and commissions would reduce the future profitability of the business.

Buyers should prepare a number of different financial projections to determine if it is reasonable to expect they would be able to generate enough revenue from the business to meet their goals.

Generally speaking, the higher the risk, the lower the purchase price.

SUMMARY

Anyone can be a potential buyer for the right opportunity, provided they can afford to pay for it.

However, selling is generally a "once in a lifetime" event. We'll discuss the seller's perspective in the next chapter.

❸
FOR SELLERS AND
POTENTIAL SELLERS ONLY

*"Every successful man I have heard of has done
the best he could with conditions as he found them,
and not waited until next year for better."*

Edgar Watson Howe

In order for a transaction to happen, there needs to be both a buyer and a seller. While some financial advisors say "I'll sell when I'm offered $500,000 or $1,000,000," others say they enjoy the business too much to ever leave. The truth is no one stays in the business forever.

In this chapter we will consider whether or not you have the right to sell your practice, and ways to prepare your business to get the best price.

IS IT YOURS TO SELL?

"Do the clients belong to the firm or the advisor?"

Every potential seller needs to determine whether or not they have the right to sell their client assets. Some advisors have signed agreements with their firm that clearly prohibit them from selling their client assets to another advisor, or taking their clients with them to another firm. Other firms and agreements are silent on the issue of client ownership.

Here is a sampling of how some firms deal with the issue of "who owns the client?"

1. The firm owns the clients. The financial advisor is an employee of the firm with no rights to sell the client assets or records when they terminate their employment. When they leave the firm, these advisors leave behind their clients and the client assets are divided among other advisors at the firm. The residual value of the client assets to the advisor is zero.

2. The firm owns the clients, but also recognizes the marketing effort that goes into building a client base. The firm's compensation program may include paying the retiring advisor a bonus equal to one times their annual revenues for assisting with the transition of the client assets to another advisor at the firm.

3. The advisor has the right to sell or transfer their client assets, but the firm retains the right to try to preserve those assets within the firm. If the advisor leaves the firm, what happens in practice is that the clients are assigned to other advisors within the firm (for ongoing service) who then compete with the leaving advisor.

4. The advisor has the right to sell or transfer their client assets to any advisor of their choice—and the firm will not solicit the clients.

5. The advisor has the right to sell or transfer their client assets, but only to a financial advisor or planner working for the same firm (or an affiliated firm) and operating under the same agreement.

6. The advisor has the right to sell or transfer their client assets, but the firm or franchise may retain the right to "accept" or "approve" any potential buyer before a deal can be finalized.

Where the fit is right, it's my personal belief that it can pay for firms to assist in the transition of client assets to a successor advisor at the same firm. Because succession planning can help retain client assets within the firm, it is ultimately good for the firm and its distributors. Assisting with the sale of client assets (or the "transition of clients") between advisors within the same firm or network of firms may include developing internal formulas or guidelines, establishing an internal registry, or even assisting with financing.

As a potential seller you should carefully review your agreements to determine if you have the right to sell or transfer your book of business to anyone of your choice and whether or not you are restricted by any non-compete or non-solicit agreement.

TIP *Dig out any agreements you have signed with your firm. Make a copy, read it and highlight the areas related to client ownership, non-solicitation, client files and termination. It may be helpful to have your lawyer review it with you.*

There is no value in attempting to sell your practice to anyone if you cannot guarantee it is yours to sell.

Ultimately, it is the client who owns the client assets, and in their eyes they are not commodities to be bought, sold or even transferred to another advisor. They are consumers of financial services and advice and they decide whom they will work with.

TIP *In some provinces, the value of the practice is considered in the calculation of a settlement for divorce/separation purposes, even when the financial advisor has signed a contract with their firm that prohibits or restricts him or her from selling or transferring those clients.*

WHY DO YOU WANT TO SELL?

Buyers will want to know why you are selling your practice. There are all sorts of reasons. Maybe it's time to retire, or do something else. Perhaps you are moving to another part of the country and need to sell your book of business here to start there. Maybe you don't want to deal with the ever-increasing compliance and ongoing professional development. Perhaps you find fee-based compensation to be less thrilling than commission and miss the highs that came from placing a sale.

Your reasons for selling may affect the potential buyer's interest in your business and the price they will pay. Knowing why you are selling might help them structure terms in their offer to meet your needs. Even when a house is up for sale, the potential buyers look to why it is being sold—transfer, death, foreclosure, divorce, etc.

If you are selling because you are losing clients or are unable to make a go of the business for any reason, that reason could be considered a material fact. You need to disclose all material facts to the potential buyer. A material fact, would include facts that had the buyer known those facts, they would not have bought the practice, or would have offered a significantly different price.

TIP *If there are potential problems with your business, obtain legal advice to determine if you are required to disclose that information.*

WHY SELL?

Why are you interested in selling your business? (Check all that apply)

❑ Time to retire

❑ I just don't want to do this anymore

❑ Increasing competition

❑ Clients are more demanding

❑ Refocusing on one line of business, such as insurance and selling off the mutual fund side

❑ Health issues

❑ Family issues

❑ Been approached by a potential buyer with an attractive proposal

❑ Moving to another region

❑ Reaction to changes occurring in the industry

❑ Other business opportunities

❑ Disability

❑ Death in the family

❑ Not as much fun as it used to be

❑ There must be an easier way to make a living

❑ Bored with the business

❑ I don't like the changes my firm is going through

❑ Don't want to deal with ever-increasing compliance regulations

❑ Don't want to have to take any more courses or get a designation

❑ Burnout

❑ Finding it harder to make a living

❑ Other

WHAT ARE YOU SELLING?

Are you selling a business or a personal service practice? I believe it's possible to run a personal service practice as a profitable business. One lawyer told their client, who was selling a personal service practice, that they "could be selling nothing more than their client list. There is no guarantee that any of your clients will move to the new advisor."

What are you selling? It is a client list? Client assets? An introduction to your clients? A guaranteed revenue stream?

WHAT ARE YOU SELLING?

(Check all that apply)

❏ Client list

❏ Client assets

❏ Prospect list

❏ Revenues

❏ Work in progress

❏ Profits

❏ Potential profitability

❏ Other business assets (real estate, furniture and equipment, etc.)

Client assets and other assets of the business are valued differently. If you have real estate and other non-client assets, you may get a better price if you sell them separately, than trying to find a potential buyer who is interested in both the client assets and the non-client assets.

Where the value of the client assets is relatively small, the business may not have a sale value. Rather than selling the client assets, the advisor may want to find someone to take over the clients, so they can exit gracefully from the business.

WHAT ARE YOU LOOKING FOR IN A BUYER?

You should be looking for someone who is willing and able to provide your clients with the service and advice they have come to expect. Not every potential buyer will be right for the needs of your clients. Others are "just looking"—not serious buyers.

In addition to being able to pay the right price for your practice and agree to your terms, there are other characteristics to look for in a potential buyer that will allow you to exit from your role as the clients' advisor.

Ask yourself if the potential buyer:

- shares values similar to your own
- has an investment philosophy similar to your own
- has the right professional credentials, experience and education
- is someone you will be able to work with through the transition period
- would commit to make the effort needed to enhance retention
- has the financial resources to pay for the business, or if they are asking you to take back financing, can afford to make the scheduled payments
- has reasonable expectations
- has a clean track record
- is someone you would let manage your own investments

TIP   *If you can, pick your successor and think of the transaction as a succession plan rather than a deal. If you do it well, few clients will even ask if there was any financial arrangement between you and the buyer.*

PREPARING YOUR BUSINESS FOR SALE

If you are in the planning stage, you have the opportunity to maximize the value of your business, both for yourself as long as you want to be an advisor, and its ultimate sale price.

The key determinant of the value of your business is how well it is run and how profitable it is. To get a better price, you need to run a better business. To run a better business, you need to follow good practice management and focus on:

1. increasing your revenues
2. running a more efficient practice

3. building loyal client relationships
4. managing a diversified product mix.

Where two practices have the same assets under administration and revenues, buyers should be willing to pay more for the more profitable business. And while you are managing the business, don't you deserve to make more money?

Increase Your Revenues

Increasing your revenues, along with managing your expenses, will contribute to your bottom-line profitability. At certain points in the market cycle, this is easier said than done. There are two main ways to increase revenues — one, work with more clients, and two, earn more revenue per client.

Work With More Clients

To work with more clients, you have to attract them through your marketing efforts, building your profile, and obtaining more referrals from existing clients and centres of influence.

Earn More Revenue Per Client

To earn more revenue per client, you can consider:

- moving up-market to clients who have larger portfolios to manage
- attracting more assets from your existing clients by taking a financial planning approach to your practice
- adding more products to your practice so you can cross-sell to your existing clients
- pruning clients who are not profitable, or define an appropriate level of service for them. Every practice has some great and not-so-great clients but buyers are not interested in paying for dead weight.

Run A More Efficient Practice

Certainly, reducing expenses, where appropriate, can increase your profitability. You might use lower-cost resources, such as staff or technology, for tasks that do not require your level of expertise. Many financial advisors and planners have implemented good marketing practices, but have not yet implemented procedures to run the practice more efficiently.

If you are in the early years of your business, your expenses may be on the high side because of your investment in marketing. If you are independent and more established, your expenses, not including your own compensation, may settle at around 30 to 35 percent of revenues; less if you are with a full-service firm (because some of the expenses are reflected in the production grid).

Some costs can be reduced for an immediate impact on profits. Other costs might increase in the short-term, but increase the profitability of your business down the road, such as an investment in software. If you are looking to sell your practice soon, focus on those changes that would increase the profitability of the business sooner rather than later, without compromising the overall value of your practice.

TIP   *Don't just cut expenses. Instead, analyze your expenses in relation to current revenues and the impact you expect them to have on future revenues and profits.*

Build Deep, Loyal Client Relationships

Having strong client relationships reduces the level of client attrition and means your clients are more likely to follow your lead when you introduce them to your successor.

To build deep, loyal client relationships, clients need to have reasonable expectations as to the role of the advisor.

SAMPLE INCOME AND EXPENSE STATEMENT

Income

Investment trailer/service fees	$100,000	
Insurance commissions—first year	70,000	
Investment commissions—first year	70,000	
Fees tied to size of account	65,000	
Insurance renewal fees	50,000	
Financial planning fees (hourly)	12,000	
Other	1,000	
Gross Income		$368,000
Production Grid (30% withheld)		110,400
Income after Production Grid		$257,600

Expenses

Owner compensation	$100,000	
Staff compensation	55,000	
Rent	12,000	
Client appreciation events	6,000	
Employee benefits	6,000	
Leasing costs	6,000	
Vehicle expenses	6.000	
Prospecting events	5,000	
Entertainment	5,000	
Office expenses	5,000	
Advertising	4,000	
Marketing costs	4,000	
Insurance (overhead, car, etc.)	4,000	
Professional services	3,000	
Phone/fax/data services	2,400	
Payroll costs (EI, CPP, etc.)	2,200	
Professional memberships	2,695	
Travel	2,000	
Other expenses	2,000	
Computer repairs/maintenance	1,200	
Utilities	1,200	
Amortization	1,000	
Professional development	600	
Fees paid to regulators	500	
		$236,795
Net Income Before Taxes		$ 20,805

Clients also require great service and a level of advice appropriate to their needs. This includes letting them know what you do for them, doing it, and then reminding them over and over again of the value of working with a financial advisor.

Watch Your Product Mix

Your clients' investment performance affects the value of your practice. Market growth can contribute to your revenues and the level of client satisfaction.

Proprietary products tie the client to the firm. If the buyer works for the same firm as you do, this would not be an issue, unless they are planning to leave the firm in the near future. If the buyer works for an external firm, they would not be willing to pay for these client assets.

Some buyers are looking primarily for recurring revenues and would discount all commission income. Other buyers are looking for a diversified mix of revenue from both commission and recurring fees.

AUDITING YOUR BUSINESS

Sellers should audit their own practice. If you were selling a house, you would go through the house to ensure there were no problems that would reduce the price a buyer would be willing to pay. You'd also do what you could to spruce it up so it showed in the best possible light. You would profile its features and get the housekeeping up-to-date.

It is working *on* the business rather than working *in* the business that increases the bottom-line profits — the value most buyers of other types of businesses are interested in.

Profile Your Practice

To profile your practice for a potential buyer, think of the features a buyer would looking for. The buyer would want to know the qualitative and quantitative aspects of your business, including all its sources of revenues, its expenses, the client assets, a profile of the client base, as well as a profile of yourself and the way you manage the practice.

You can analyze the financial aspects of your business using the worksheets and checklists provided throughout the book, as well as consider the factors that can increase or decrease the purchase price found in Chapter 6. This information can also be used for the preliminary discussions with interested buyers.

Later in the due diligence process, you will be asked to provide source documents to support your preliminary information, such as your production reports for investments and insurance, trailer fee reports from each investment company, audited financial statements for the last two or three years (where they exist), asset listings, and commission statements. The buyer may also ask you to disclose your income and expense statement, and if it is relevant to your business structure, copies of your tax return.

Suppose you were a potential buyer looking at your own business. Knowing the hours you work, the types of investments your clients hold, the value of the assets under management and the money you take home, how much would you be prepared to pay for it?

TIP *Once you have identified opportunities to improve your business, adjust your business and marketing plans to address them, starting with those that are the easiest to implement and would have the greatest impact on the value of your business.*

Make Sure Your Housekeeping Is Up-To-Date

Be sure your client files are organized and that all client paperwork is up-to-date.

If you are a private corporation, also make sure your corporate books and financial statements are up-to-date.

TIP   *If you are contemplating selling your practice, start plan-ning three to five years in advance to maximize its future value.*

WHAT ELSE DO YOU WANT FROM THE DEAL?

Sellers also have to consider:

- when they want to sell the business. Is it now, a few years out or not for many years?
- their target selling price
- whether or not they will offer vendor-take-back financing
- how long they want to stay involved with the business after the sale.

WHEN DO YOU REALLY WANT TO LEAVE THE BUSINESS?

After the deal closes, when would you like to be completely out of the business (i.e. not involved with compliance and/or transition issues)?

❑ Less than 6 months

❑ 6 months to a year

❑ 1 to 3 years

❑ 3 to 5 years

❑ more than 5 years

Sellers looking to retire may be interested in easing them-selves into full retirement. They may be willing to stay active in the business, but in a reduced way, in exchange for a higher sale price. Others may be willing to accept a lower price if it means they can be out of the business more quickly.

SUMMARY

A number of deals don't happen for a variety of reasons, even when a potential buyer and potential seller have found each other. Some sellers discover they are not ready to leave the business and give up the annual income. Others find they only want to sell off their smaller clients so they can turn their focus to their larger clients – and work fewer hours without taking a significant drop in their income.

Many financial advisory practices would be classified more as a "professional service" than a "business." The valuation of a professional service firm, such as a chiropractic or dental practice, is around one times the average annual gross revenues of the practice. In the case of a dental practice, there is no guarantee the seller's patients will become the buyer's patients. The potential buyer knows they might be able to open a practice across the street from the retiring dentist and attract those patients over time through their marketing efforts. These types of factors put a natural cap on the price any buyer would be willing to pay. Similarly, potential buyers of financial advisory and planning practices look at the revenues of the practice and assess whether or not they believe this revenue is something they would be willing to pay for.

For the motivated buyer and seller, the next step is to determine what the practice is worth, given its strengths and weaknesses, current and potential profitability, as well as the outlook for the industry.

4

METHODS OF
VALUING A PRACTICE

*"Profit is the product of labor plus
capital multiplied by management.
You can hire the first two.
The last must be inspired."*
Fost

There is no magic formula for valuing or pricing a financial advisory or planning practice, nor is it easy to compare the value of your practice to other practices since the details of actual transactions are generally not made public.

The concept for valuing a financial advisory or planning practice boils down to "what's it worth?" or more accurately, "what's someone willing to pay?"

The perceived worth is different to the buyer and the seller. The buyer focuses primarily on what the practice is worth to-day — the business "as is" — and the seller often wants to include the potential profitability of the business — what the business *could* be worth. There are many rumours about the price sellers are receiving for their business, ranging from next to nothing to over ten times the free cash flow.

In some circles, a small professional practice or service business does not have a significant sale value because:

- there is no certainty that the seller's client relationship will transfer to the buyer
- it is relatively easy to build the practice from scratch without requiring a significant capital investment.

While there are various methodologies for valuing different types of businesses, many of these methods have limited application to the financial advisory or planning practice. Since most financial advisory practices have little in the way of capital assets, real estate or inventories, the book or cost method of valuing businesses is of little use. The nature of the business means there is little or no liquidation value. There is no value if the client accounts and loyalties don't transfer to the new advisor. However, the personal referral of the seller and goodwill, both intangible assets can have sizable value — provided the business can be transferred to the buyer as a "going concern."

THE FIVE MOST COMMON METHODS OF VALUATION

The five most common methods used to value a book of business are based on:
- the size of the book of business or assets under management
- historical commission and fee income
- the historical annual recurring revenues the business has generated
- the revenues the business will generate, or actual revenues received
- the business's bottom-line profitability, or its free cash flow.

TIP   *Even if your firm has guidelines or formulas in place to facilitate succession planning, each buyer and seller has to assess for him or herself if those guidelines work for their practice.*

The valuation methods are the starting point for determining the selling price for the practice. Other factors also affect the price, such as the nature of the business, asset retention and financing arrangements. These other factors will be addressed in later chapters.

The valuation method used can be as complex or as simple as the buyer and seller want to make it. But regardless of the formula the buyer and seller agree to use, the selling price is ultimately based on what the seller hopes to get and what the buyer is willing to pay.

Some transactions establish the purchase price up front; others agree on a formula that will be used to determine the purchase price, depending on future revenues or retention. Still other agreements establish a minimum price or include a non-refundable deposit, plus offer a bonus or adjust the final price upwards if certain targets or benchmarks are met. Setting a minimum price ensures the seller receives some value for selling their practice as a going concern and ensures they are not just handing the buyer an opportunity to market to their clients.

Each method bases the price on a particular variable of the business, and applies a multiple or factor. As a rule of thumb, think of these five methods of using factors of ½, 1, 2, 2.5, and 3 respectively for a mutual fund practice. As with any rule of thumb, this one may or may not be helpful, or even relevant to your particular situation, once all the variables have been considered.

TIP *The larger the factor or multiple used, the higher the purchase price, and the greater the business risk to the buyer.*

When the market value of client assets were increasing at a rate of 8 to 12 percent a year, some buyers were willing to pay prices based on higher multiples, already factoring in some of the future growth of the stock market. Today, even though the number of potential buyers is greater than the number of advisors interested in selling their practice, the pricing of financial practices has returned to the mid or lower end of the multiple range. The price at the upper end will be capped by the buyer answering the question: "Could I acquire the types of clients I want, with less risk, through marketing rather than buying this practice?" As it becomes more costly to build a practice from scratch, a buyer might be willing to pay a higher premium.

TIP *When stock markets are weak, buyers will focus on today's profits and tend to discount the potential for profits, pushing down sale prices. When stock markets are strong, buyers may be willing to pay a premium for future profits.*

The buyer has to ensure the price they offer bears some relation to the current and future profits they expect to earn once they acquire the business. They will adjust the factor or multiple almost intuitively to factor in what they expect to earn from the book of business — and how much money and time they are willing to invest before they earn profits for themselves.

TIP *Buyers should consider how many years it would take to recover the cost of buying the client assets.*

When you hear that someone was able to sell their practice using a relatively high multiple, it doesn't automatically follow that they received a higher selling price. You need to look beyond the multiple and consider the other variables that were used in setting the price, such as did they use historical or actual revenues and whether or not they used income or revenue figures before or after applying the grid, to determine if it is better or worse than other deals.

Let's look at how these basic valuation methods work and some of the advantages and disadvantages of each.

ASSETS UNDER MANAGEMENT

Assets under management (AUM), or the total value of the client assets the financial advisor or planner manages, has long been a status symbol among financial advisors and planners. Recently, there has been an interest on gathering assets that have the potential to be turned into fee-generating assets.

Using the AUM method, the purchase price is based on the current market value of the assets under management, times some multiple. The more assets under management, the higher the price.

The multiple ranges from $\frac{1}{2}$ to two times or more.

Suppose a practice has $50 million in mutual fund assets under management, and the buyer and seller agree to use a factor of $\frac{1}{2}$ or 50 basis points. The selling price of the business would be set at $250,000.

AUM VALUATION METHOD

Assets Under Management		Multiple Used	Purchase Price
Bonds	$20 million		
Stocks	15		
Mutual Funds	15		
	$50 million	50 bps	$250,000

I call this the "ego based" valuation method, where the seller says something like "I've worked hard to gather all these valuable assets. Pay me for them." But today's buyers are focusing on the business part of the practice, not just the size of the practice. Which would you prefer? A practice with $50 million in assets under management that earns $150,000 of profits annually, or a practice with $40 million in AUM that earns $200,000 of profits annually?

Used alone, the AUM method bears no relation to the profits the business might generate, nor does it factor in either the nature of the client assets or retention of those assets. To factor in client retention, the buyer may want to use a lower multiple. However, if the buyer expects they will be able to convert the client assets to investments that pay a higher fee (provided it is in the clients' best interest) to increase future profits, the buyer might be prepared to use a higher multiple

Basing a sale price solely on gross assets under administration or gross revenues reminds me of those Internet companies that focused on attracting "eyeballs" because they expected them to be worth something someday. Some of the assets may not generate much in the way of revenues and may even be a drain on the bottom-line profits, because of the cost to service them. As many technology investors have found out, if the price paid for a company is not linked to its profitability, it might only be a great idea whose time may or may not arrive.

Advantages
- The method of calculating the price is simple.
- Price is determined upfront.
- Numbers are easy to verify from corporate reports or mutual fund holding reports.

Disadvantages
- No relation to the revenue the practice generates.
- No relation to the profitability of the business.
- Attrition is not factored in.

HISTORICAL COMMISSION AND FEE INCOME

Many transactions have based the purchase price on the annual income the practice earned for the seller. Some deals have looked at the income earned over the last twelve months; others at the average income earned over the last three years.

Using the historical commission and fee income method, the purchase price is based on previous earned revenue times some multiple. The higher the annual income, the higher the price. Like the AUM method, this method establishes a purchase price that may bear no relation to the profits the business generates, nor does it factor in the retention of client assets, the nature of those assets and the mix of commission and fee income.

TIP   *Large commission payments may be difficult to duplicate going forward.*

The multiple used ranges from 1 to 1¼ times or more. Where a high percentage of the income came from one-time commissions, the buyer may want to use a lower multiple.

Suppose a practice earned $210,000 last year in commission and fee income, and the buyer and seller agree to use a factor of 1. The starting point for establishing a selling price of the business would be $210,000.

HISTORICAL COMMISSION AND FEE INCOME

Income		Multiple Used	Purchase Price
Commission	$200,000		
Fee	$100,000		
	$300,000		
After the grid (70%)	$210,000	1	$210,000

The buyer and the seller both have to consider if:
- the income can be duplicated going forward
- the client base can continue to generate a similar level of commission income
- commissions will continue to be one of the preferred method of compensation.

Advantages
- The method of calculating the price is simple.
- Numbers are easy to verify from income and/or commission reports.

Disadvantages
- Does not directly consider whether or not the commission income can be repeated.
- No relation to the future revenues of the practice.
- No relation to the profitability of the business.
- Attrition is not factored in.

HISTORICAL ANNUAL RECURRING REVENUES (HARR)

Under the historical annual recurring revenue (HARR) method for valuing a practice, the selling price is based on only those revenues that recur, or are expected to recur, such as fee and trailer income, renewal premiums and perhaps commissions from pre-authorized or automatic savings programs (PAC). One-time fee-for-service financial planning income or consulting would not be considered recurring revenue unless the fees paid by the client are part of a long-term retainer agreement or letter of engagement.

The recurring revenue method does not normally include one-time commission income that can vary widely from year to year. Just one or two big commission-based deals can make the practice look to be worth a great deal more than it really is. But when the seller can demonstrate that commission income has been fairly consistent and can be expected to continue — such as commissions from PACs, RRSPs, IRAs or 401(k) contributions — the seller might negotiate that these commissions be considered recurring revenue.

The multiple used for mutual fund assets ranges from two to 2½ times or more. For insurance assets, I've heard numbers of five or more times the renewal income. Perhaps the assumption here is that insurance renewals can be considered a reliable stream of income for longer than mutual fund trailers. Some transactions use different multiples for different lines of businesses.

Suppose a practice earned $150,000 last year in recurring revenues from wrap and mutual fund assets. If the buyer and seller agree to use a factor of 2, the starting point for establishing the selling price would be $210,000.

HISTORICAL ANNUAL RECURRING REVENUE

Recurring Fee Income from		Multiple Used	Purchase Price
Mutual fund service			
/trailer fees	$ 75,000		
Segregated funds	25,000		
Wrap assets fees	$ 50,000		
	$150,000		
After the grid (70%)	$105,000	2	$210,000

Advantages
- Price is determined upfront.
- Calculating the price is relatively simple.
- Numbers extracted from firm or third-party reports.

Disadvantages
- No relation to the profitability of the business.
- Costs of running the business not factored in.
- Attrition is not factored in.

REVENUES ACTUALLY RECEIVED (RAR)

The attrition rate, or loss of client assets, is such an issue for some buyers that they are not interested in a practice where a purchase price is established upfront based on historical revenues and/or profits generated prior to the transaction date. These potential buyers want to mitigate the potential risk related to losing clients and market performance by buying a practice where the purchase price will be based on the actual revenues they generate after the transaction. Sellers in these transactions risk not being adequately compensated for their practice, since these deals place all the risk of attrition on the seller, risk they have little control over.

Under the revenues actually received (RAR) method for valuing a practice, the selling price is based on only those revenues, after the grid, that are earned after the transaction date—on a "go forward" basis.

The multiple used for mutual fund assets ranges from 2½ to 3 times or more times the actual revenues earned. Suppose the multiple used 2½ times. The buyer may make payments every three months over two and a half years, or 10 quarters.

REVENUES ACTUALLY RECEIVED (RAR)

Actual revenues received		Multiple Used	Purchase Price
1st quarter	$ 25,000		
2nd quarter	28,000		
3rd quarter	30,000		
4th quarter	30,000		
5th quarter	28,000		
6th quarter	32,000		
7th quarter	32,000		
8th quarter	34,000		
9th quarter	36,000		
10th quarter	40,000		
Total:	$290,000		
After the grid (70%)	$203,000	2.5	$507,500

Some deals have used a two-part formula to setting the purchase price. One part of the purchase price is fixed upfront, based on historical revenues, and the other part is variable, based on revenues actually received.

While this method automatically factors in retention (if the client leaves, so does the income is generated from their account), the buyer could end up compensating the seller for work they do themselves unless the deal is carefully structured. Suppose the seller was licensed to sell mutual funds and the buyer is licensed to sell mutual funds and insurance. If the buyer did a full financial plan with each client as part of the transition process and uncovered opportunities to cross-sell life insurance to the clients, they may not want to have to pay the seller for this work.

Advantages
- Factors in client attrition.
- Financing payments can be tied to the revenues the buyer receives.

Disadvantages
- No direct link to the profitability of the practice.
- The buyer may not be compensated adequately for the added revenue they generate from working with clients.
- The seller may not be compensated for the value of the business at the time the transaction was struck.
- The seller is not compensated for marketing efforts done prior to the transaction that come to fruition after the sale.
- If the purchase price is not determined upfront (just a formula), the seller may not be able to take advantage of the tax reserve.

Income And Revenues Before Or After The Grid?

The firm's grid payout affects each advisor's bottom line. Buyers will not normally pay a seller for revenues that are kept by their firm. However, if the buyer and seller work for the same firm and are paid on the same basis after applying the grid, they could use either gross revenues or revenues after the grid as a basis for determining the purchase price, and adjust the multiple they use accordingly.

However, if the buyer and seller are paid according to different grid schedules, the buyer would want the calculations to reflect their own grid payout schedule (especially if it is lower than the seller's) or lower if they anticipate the grid payout will fall.

TIP *Buyers who do not factor in the costs of running the practice may be "buying" their own job, rather than running a profitable business.*

FREE CASH FLOW

The free cash flow (FCF) method of valuing a business links the purchase price to the historical bottom-line profits. The free cash flow method has been used to value many different types of businesses, ranging from retail business and manufacturing concerns, as well as financial advisory and planning practices.

Free cash flow looks at the business's profitability. It begins with the annual income (IBDIT) the business earns before depreciation, interest and taxes, after the grid, less the expenses and costs of operating the business, and less the income and benefits earned by the financial advisor or planner.

A multiple (which is linked to the cap rate where the cap rate = 1/multiple) is applied to the annual free cash flow for profitable financial advisory practices. While the pricing of institutional books has been based on multiples of 10 or more, the multiple used for financial advisory and planning practices generally fall between two and four. Potential buyers should be willing to pay more for the more profitable business.

Suppose a practice with $350,000 income (after-the-grid) has annual expenses of $50,000 and pays the two staff $75,000 and the advisor/owner $100,000 in salary and benefits. If the free cash flow were $125,000 and the buyer and seller agreed to use a multiple of three, the selling price would be $375,000.

FREE CASH FLOW

			Multiple Used	Purchase Price
Gross Income	$500,000			
After the grid (70% payout)		$350,000		
Less				
Seller's Salary	$100,000			
Staff Salaries	75,000			
Expenses	50,000			
	Subtotal:	$225,000		
Free Cash Flow		$125,000	3	$375,000

If a multiple of four is used, the owner may not earn any profits for themselves from the business until the end of year 4 (not including the costs of financing). If a multiple of two is used, the owner has to be prepared to run the business for two years before earning profits for themselves.

If the buyer expects profits could grow strongly, or that they could be able to gather more assets from the acquired client base, or increase profits by realizing cost savings, they may be willing to pay a higher multiple. But they don't want to overpay, in case these don't materialize.

Some sellers have considered accepting an offer with a lower multiple if it is accompanied with a potential bonus payment down the road. But buyer should also consider if they want to open their books in the future to justify the bonus (or no bonus) to the seller.

When a practice is not profitable, and does not have the potential to turn a profit, the seller could wait a long time for someone to buy it. So what about those financial advisory and planning practices that generate a good income for the advisor but do not have much in the way of profits? Some buyers will consider a book of client assets where they can see the potential for profits. In these situations, they may be willing to discount the income made by the advisor.

Reviewing The Seller's Financial Statements

It takes more work to price a business using the free cash flow numbers than using the other methods. Because the profitability numbers come from their business's own internal reports, more statements have to be reviewed and verified. The buyer may want to bring their accountant to help audit and verify the business's own financial reports.

When reviewing the seller's financial statements, the buyer and seller may make adjustments to the bottom-line profits, including the owner's income, personal expenses run through the business and the profit pattern.

Owner's income

If the seller is drawing an income that is less than the buyer would expect an advisor to make, they will adjust the seller's salary accordingly. Where the practice is very profitable, the advisor may pay themselves a generous salary, and want the salary to be adjusted, but in the opposite direction.

What income do you believe is appropriate for a good established professional financial advisor or planner? $100,000 to $250,000 a year or more? $100 to $200 an hour or more? The assumptions affect the price the buyer would pay and what the seller expects to be paid.

Suppose the average income for a financial advisor or planner is $100,000 and the seller is paying himself or herself $250,000, $150,000 might be added back into the free cash flow statement. If the seller is paying him or herself $50,000, the buyer might adjust the profit figure downwards.

		Multiple Used	Purchase Price
Gross Income $400,000			
After the grid (50% payout) $200,000			
Less			
Seller's Salary 50,000			
Staff Salaries 30,000			
Expenses 25,000			
Subtotal: $105,000			
Unadjusted Free Cash Flow	$ 95,000		
Adjust to reflect $100,000 advisor salary	(50,000)		
Free Cash Flow	$ 45,000	4	$180,000

Personal expenses

Where the seller flows personal expenses through the business, such as entertainment, car expenses or travel, the profit statement would be adjusted to more accurately reflect the profit the buyer could expect to generate.

Profits over more than one year

The potential buyer will want to assess the practice's profit patterns over a number of years, to see if they are stable, growing or declining.

Advantages
- Demonstrates the current profitability of the practice
- Price is determined upfront

Disadvantages
- Uses business's own reports
- Take additional work to audit and verify the practice's own profit/loss statements
- Difficult to use for practices with low profitability
- Difficult to use for practices selling only some client assets
- Adjustments to statements may become contentious

SUMMARY

In this chapter, we considered the value of the business based on quantitative factors including assets under management, income, revenues, expenses, profitability, as well as the potential for profits.

WHAT'S YOUR PREFERRED VALUATION METHOD?

Preferred method(s) of valuing the business (Check all that apply)

❑ Assets under management

❑ Historical commission and fee income

❑ Historical annual recurring revenue

❑ Revenues actually received

❑ Free cash flow

❑ Bonus for client assets retained

❑ Combination

❑ Don't know

Regardless of the method used to set the purchase price, buyers will focus on the profits they expect to earn from the client base. Most buyers want to be able to turn a clear profit by the 3rd or 4th year — regardless of the direction of the stock market and changes within the industry.

Some transactions set the purchase price by combining the price from different methods, or have even averaged the results of the five methods. A practice could be valued under five different methods, and come up with approximately the same selling price, depending on the makeup of the business and the rate of attrition and market growth.

Other factors affect the final purchase price, such as attrition, nature of the practice, and financing. We will explore these other factors in the following chapters.

❺

FACTORING ATTRITION INTO THE EQUATION

"Small opportunities are often the beginning of great enterprises."
Demosthenes

Client retention is a key determinant in the value of any professional practice, whether it is a legal, dental or financial advisory or planning practice. Clients are the source of the revenues the business generates.

There is no guarantee the clients will accept the succeeding professional as their own. Some attrition—how many clients and their assets might leave—is inevitable when a practice is sold. Client attrition, or shrinkage, should be anticipated and factored into the purchase price. Each buyer has to consider "how much of the loyalty, trust and goodwill the seller currently has with the clients is transferable?" The more that can be transferred to the buyer, the greater the retention of client assets.

Clients do not "belong" to the advisor or to the firm. Unless the client is locked into proprietary products, they are free to move their account to the advisor at any firm they choose.

Sometimes a change in advisor will prompt some clients to explore their options and react as if the money "is in motion."

Some clients will want to choose their own financial advisor and during transition may view your change as an opportunity to take a hard look at how they are doing and re-evaluate what has being done. If they meet another advisor who can get a foothold in the crack of uncertainty the change has opened up; the client may be lost.

TIP *Many advisors have a few clients who are "at risk" of leaving. Buyers may want to exclude any clients at risk from the calculation of the purchase price.*

WHAT IS A GOOD RETENTION RATE?

The natural attrition rate (the percentage of clients that leave their current advisor each year) seems to range from one to two percent a year. Some advisors experience a higher attrition rate within their books of business, some less. Clients choose to transfer their account to an advisor at another firm, die or move out of the area.

When I talked to advisors who changed firms and moved their books of business to the new firm, they expected that approximately 70 to 80 percent of the non-proprietary assets actually move with them—even more where the advisor was providing good advice and service. (Of course, some advisors may be happy to "lose" some of these clients.) This is one reason some firms offer a signing bonus or bridging payment when hiring experienced advisors—to help them maintain their income through the transition period.

TIP *Buyers should do financial projections based on the anticipated attrition rate, using a best case, the most likely case, as well as the worst case over the first two years.*

While some potential buyers believe an attrition rate of more than 10 percent is high, today's clients have more choice. I would suggest that any transaction where the buyer is able to retain more than 75 percent of the client assets over a three-year period adjusted for market performance had experienced good client retention.

HOW TO REDUCE CLIENT ATTRITION

Much of the value of financial advisory practice is based on the seller's goodwill. Some of this goodwill is totally dependent on the seller and is not transferable to the buyer. However, the better the fit between the seller and the buyer, the more the transaction can be seen as a succession rather than a "sale" in the eyes of the clients. A good fit, complemented with a well-thought-out transition strategy, can significantly lower the rate of client attrition.

The risk of attrition is lower in internal transactions where the buyer and the seller work for the same firm in the same office when clients can continue to receive the same level of service, advice and familiar paperwork.

TIP   *If a buyer does not believe they can retain certain client assets, he or she shouldn't pay for them! If the seller is selling the practices as an "all or none" offer, the buyer would want to use a lower multiple or factor, or structure part of the deal as a retention bonus.*

The longer the seller stays with the business, or is perceived to be involved in the business, the higher the retention—provided this does not inhibit the ability of the buyer to bond with the clients.

Is retention the responsibility of the buyer or the seller? It's the responsibility of <u>both</u> whenever a practice is sold as a going concern. Both the seller and the buyer need to commit to do what is reasonable to retain the client assets. The value of the business to the buyer is based on his or her ability to retain the assets, which is directly related to:

- how well the seller prepares the clients for the transition
- how loyal the clients were to the seller

- whether or not the clients like the buyer
- whether or not the buyer commits to work with the clients to earn their loyalty and trust.

With proper client care and communication, many clients do choose to stay with the successor advisor, as long as it appears to be in their own best interest.

SOME WAYS TO FACTOR ATTRITION INTO THE PURCHASE PRICE

No buyer wants to pay for client assets that disappear, for whatever reason, shortly after the transaction is closed.

The best transactions find a balance between paying the seller for their business without requiring the buyer to pay for assets that they, through no fault of their own, are not able to retain.

Here are some ways buyers and sellers have attempted to factor attrition into the final purchase price.

1. Where the purchase price is to be determined upfront, the buyer may discount the purchase price by using a lower factor or multiple, anticipating a certain level of attrition.

2. Rather than using historical recurring revenues, they have based the purchase price solely on the revenues generated from client assets after the transaction date

    While this method may be the most desirable to the buyer, it is not the most desirable to the seller who has little or no direct control over:
    - the relationship the buyer establishes with the clients
    - market conditions after the purchase date
    - the effort the buyer puts into retaining the clients.

    This method does not require the buyer to put their best efforts into working with the clients. Suppose the buyer finds himself in the middle of a messy divorce shortly after the deal is signed and is not able to focus on retaining the clients. The seller would not receive an appropriate purchase price.

3. In addition to the base purchase price, the buyer offers a bonus payment based on assets under management, where retention targets are achieved 12 to 24 months after the purchase. However, basing a retention bonus on a longer period of time could be unfair to the seller because they have less influence with the clients the more time passes.

TIP *Where a seller agrees to be paid a bonus if the buyer achieves a target level of retention, be sure to factor in market conditions using market benchmarks. Suppose a bonus is to be paid to the seller only if the value of client assets retained is 90 percent of the value on the closing date. If the market value of the assets are down due to market conditions, a seller might not receive the appropriate bonus, even where the client assets had been retained.*

4. A price adjustment clause in the purchase and sale agreement to deal with specific accounts "at risk" of transferring out, such as those accounts that have indicated to the seller they are dissatisfied.

5. A price adjustment clause in the purchase and sale agreement that reflects the actual revenues earned by the buyer over a predetermined period (such as the first 12 months after closing).

SUMMARY

Advisors don't own their clients. The client owns the client assets and decides who will be their financial advisor or planner. Client retention can be enhanced by giving the clients a reason to stay.

⑥
FACTORS THAT INCREASE/DECREASE THE PURCHASE PRICE

"I do not believe you can do today's job with yesterday's methods and be in business tomorrow."
Nelson Jackson

The final purchase price of a financial advisory or planning practice may bear little relation to the seller's target price.

While the methods of valuing a practice in Chapter 4 can be used to establish an initial price for the practice, there are a number of factors that could increase or decrease the value of the practice to the buyer — and what they would be willing to offer the seller. These factors include, but are not limited to, those related to the practice's revenues and profitability, the types of the investments in the client portfolios, the nature of the client base and the potential synergies the buyer may be able to realize after the sale.

Throughout this chapter, we will look at some of the factors to consider related to the clients and their assets, and whether or not they tend to discount the price the buyer might be willing to pay or pay the seller a premium for their business. How much these factors would affect the final purchase price is part of the negotiation process.

The Worksheets in the Appendix can be used to help determine if there is a good match between the buyer's and seller's practice. In this chapter, I've included short checklists for some of the factors that buyers can use to assess how some of these factors relate to the business they are considering buying (and by sellers to assess their own business).

If the seller is also selling non-client assets or intangible items, these could be negotiated separately, or as part of the overall transaction.

GENERAL FACTORS

The practice that is sold as a going concern will attract the best price. A practice in distress or one where the seller has outstanding liability issues will sell for less because there is more risk of losing clients.

Of course, the purchase price is tempered by what the buyer is willing to pay and what the seller is willing to accept. There seems to be a natural cap on the top price a reasonable buyer would pay for the business — around three to four times the annual net profits.

Decrease
❑ What the buyer is willing to pay

❑ Outstanding compliance issues or complaints

❑ Forced sale (death, disability, etc.)

❑ Practice in distress or decline

❑ Seller has more credentials and experience than the buyer

Increase
❑ What the seller is willing to accept

❑ Seller and buyer have been working together and both have relationships with clients

❑ Practice is run as a business with systems and procedures

Where the seller and buyer have been working together, perhaps as associates or partners, and both have established positive relationships with the client, retention of clients and their assets can be expected to be higher.

In the situation where the seller has more credentials and experience than the buyer, the advisors need to position the transaction so that the clients don't feel they are getting a less qualified advisor. Sometimes, having the seller assist for longer during the transition period can provide the reassurance the clients need—and provide the buyer with a mentor for a period of time.

It's a given that a practice with well-documented client files, with details of all correspondence, a written financial plan and an investment policy statement and asset mix for each client would command a higher price than one which is disorganized and lacks systemized processes.

REVENUES AND PROFITABILITY

Buyers want steady or growing cash flow, not liabilities and expenses, from a well-diversified client base.

Decrease

- ❑ Fee-based business during negative market conditions
- ❑ Revenues based mainly on commission income
- ❑ Declining profitability
- ❑ Significant number of non-profitable clients (dead weight)
- ❑ Income concentrated (in a few families, COI referrals, etc.)

Increase

❏ Large percentage of income from recurring revenue from clients where the advisor is perceived to be adding value

❏ Untapped potential for revenue growth

❏ Stable or growing revenues

❏ Stable or falling expenses

❏ Where the business includes overrides or a portion of the revenues generated by other advisors or planners

Concentration

Earning more than 5 to 10 percent of the revenues from any one client family, friends and family, or any one referral source creates a concentration risk. If the buyer is unable to retain these key accounts, the business the buyer receives could be very different from the one they thought they were buying.

TIP　*Examine the revenues that come from the top 15 clients or more for concentration.*

Commission Versus Fee Income

While there is much debate on the fee versus commission compensation issue, the matter may boil down to "do the clients perceive that they are receiving value from working with a financial advisor or planner?"

Other Sources Of Revenue

Some businesses provide the owner with additional sources of revenue, such as a portion of the revenue generated by other advisors or planners in the firm which would add a premium to the purchase price.

Revenue And Profit Pattern

Revenues and profits can be growing, shrinking or stable. Buyers will pay more for revenues and profits that are stable or growing.

Some practices have very little potential for future revenues and profits and sell for a discounted price, where:

- the seller has 100 percent of the client assets under administration
- the seller has met both the investment and the insurance needs of the clients
- clients have no new money to invest

Direction Of Fees And Payouts

If the buyer believes that trailer fees and grid payouts will be falling, they would discount the purchase price to reflect the lower future income.

TIP *Ask the seller if they know of any reason why future revenues or profits might be significantly different than today. They might tell you of a key client who is about to transfer their accounts or a long-term team member who is leaving.*

CLIENT ASSETS

The buyer wants to pay for assets that are stable will look for investments with features that contribute to their stability, such as years still remaining on the deferred sales schedule or insurance products with guarantees the client would not want to give up, or investments that have penalties if the client were to sell and move them. Some buyers even consider locked-in RRSPs to be relatively stable accounts because many clients do not realize how easy they are to move.

Decrease

❑ Poor investment decisions

❑ No-load investments that are easy to sell

❑ Proprietary assets

❑ Assets in RRIF/pension accounts

Increase

❑ Mutual funds with 3+ years remaining in DSC schedule

❑ Segregated funds with 3+ years remaining in guarantee period

❑ Life insurance policies

❑ Balanced investment portfolios

❑ Advice-based investments versus transaction-based

❑ Locked-in RRSPs

Poor Investment Decisions

Poor investment recommendations could negatively affect the purchase price if they affect more than a handful of clients. For example, many buyers do not want to deal with the issues often related to limited partnership investments. Review the types of investments the seller has recommended.

Assessing The Revenue Versus The Profitability Per Client

Whether you are building a business one client at a time or buying a book of clients, your goal is to end up with a practice that consists primarily of profitable clients (you're running a business, not volunteering your services). With some clients, you have the work without the reward.

It's been said time and time again that advisors typically make 80 percent of their revenue from 20 percent of their clients. Regardless of whether the breakdown is 80/20 or 70/30, a buyer should know if the practice they are considering has enough profitable clients—and not be expected to pay for the clients that are not profitable.

TIP *Many advisors have focused on gathering assets, rather than on gathering assets (and clients) that pay them for providing quality service and advice.*

EXAMPLE:

Suppose your staff receive a compensation package worth $25 an hour, your hourly rate is $100 an hour, and that you will be paying the seller based on the revenues you actually receive over 30 months.

How much will it cost you to service each client if the average client account is $70,000 and you earn a one percent annual fee (less 30% that goes to your firm). You don't expect to receive much in the way of additional assets in the first year.

Revenues Generated

Fees paid $70,000 @ 1%		$700
Less 30% kept by the firm		210
Net revenues		$490

Value of your time to service client in year 1

Prepare for initial meeting	½ hrs	$ 50
Initial meeting	1½ hrs	150
Updating the financial plan, etc. 1 hr		100
Staff's time	3 hrs	75
Second meeting	1 hr	100
2 phone calls		50
% of other expenses*		50
		$575
	Net loss in the first year	($ 85)

*Also consider the cost of licensing, compliance, continuing education, liability insurance, client appreciation programs, the cost of financing the purchase of the client, declining market values, market appreciation, falling payouts, income tax, etc.

When reviewing the profile of the clients, consider:

- how much revenue each client generates
- how profitable each client is
- for the clients with little or no current profitability, whether or not there is strong future potential.

Remember, it's quality, not quantity that counts.

To assess the profitability per client, compare the cost of servicing the client with the revenues generated.

Some advisors have learned the hard way that there can be a lot of dead weight in someone else's practice — clients where the ongoing revenues do not cover the cost to serve them, with little or no potential for future investments.

CLIENT BASE

Don't let the number of million dollar accounts turn your head. The larger the size of the client account, the more difficult it may be to retain them.

Decrease

- ❑ Investments in limited partnerships
- ❑ Elderly client base
- ❑ More than 300 client families
- ❑ Clients who have had little or no contact from the advisor in the last 6 months

Increase

- ❑ Strong client loyalty
- ❑ Clients who have been with the seller for more than 3 years
- ❑ Clients relate well to team members

Client Loyalty

As a general rule, the longer the advisor/client relationship, the stronger the client loyalty. Clients who have been working with the seller for three or more years are likely to be more loyal than those who have been working with the seller for just a few months.

Strong client loyalty can enhance the retention of client assets, provided the seller can offer the buyer a strong endorsement. However, if a number of large clients are highly dependent on receiving the seller's personal attention and are not used to working with a team member, this loyalty could turn into a negative factor.

Elderly Client Base

An investment business with an elderly client base may have limited potential for future investments, as well as a higher risk of asset attrition due to death.

On the other hand, an elderly client base that is well insured may offer the potential for future investments where the family members are beneficiaries of the life insurance proceeds (and are also clients of the seller).

POTENTIAL SYNERGIES

While sellers might want the buyer to pay for potential synergies the buyer may be able to realize after the sale (after all, that wouldn't be possible without their clients!), they should not be expected to be paid for additional income generated by the buyer, such as from:
- offering clients a larger range of products. For example, what potential exists for insurance clients to become investment clients or vice versa?
- gathering assets from the existing clients by providing them with a deeper level of advice.

MORE QUESTIONS FOR EVERY POTENTIAL BUYER TO CONSIDER

Is this a business you would buy if the price were right?

Have you valued the business using all the different formulas: assets under management, historical commission and fee income, historical annual recurring revenue, actual revenues received, and free cash flow?

Is the price fair and reasonable?

Will you be able to generate enough income to pay the seller for the client assets?

When do you expect to break even on the transaction?

Will buying the practice give you better results than investing the same dollars in a strategic marketing program?

Have you used conservative assumptions in your financial projections?

Is the seller's way of doing business and client base compatible with your own?

Where clients have been referred by strategic centres of influences or alliances, are those strategic relationships transferable?

Will you be able to integrate the new clients into your existing processes or will you be managing them as a business within a business?

Have you estimated the work required to meet all the new clients?

If the buyer and seller work for different firms, is the seller willing to move to the buyer's firm and bring the clients over to it before leaving the business?

Have you verified all the numbers related to the practice, including revenues, expenses, profits, assets, etc.?

What are your three biggest concerns about buying this practice?

The buyer may also be able to realize economies of scale or operating efficiencies, such as those that might occur when the buyer can easily integrate the clients into their own client management system.

Strategic buyers may be willing to pay a higher price and have deeper pockets than a marketing buyer because they expect to create synergy or larger economies of scale by eliminating duplication of processes, overhead, etc.

SUMMARY

There are a number of factors related to the clients and their assets that affect the price a buyer would be willing to pay.

When assessing the opportunity, some buyers may find it helpful to consider "is the seller's business a good investment?" Just as you would consider a number of factors before recommending any investment to your clients, you should base your decision to buy or not to buy any particular practice on a number of factors.

For example, before buying the stock of a particular company, you would, among other things, consider that company's:

- annual profits
- profit growth
- annual revenues
- management
- current stock price
- products and services

as well as the environment in which it operates.

Similarly, when valuing a financial advisory or planning practice, buyers should consider the practice's annual profit, its potential for growth and annual revenues, as well as the quality of its management and the asking price. Paying too much for any business can be an expensive business error.

If the buyer and the seller both like what they've seen and heard up to this stage, the next step is to work out the details needed to finance and finalize the deal.

SHOW ME THE MONEY!
PAYING FOR THE BUSINESS

*"Financial rewards follow accomplishment,
they don't precede it."*
Harry F. Banks

While sellers would like 100 percent of the purchase price in cash upfront, if they could get it; buyers would prefer to make interest-free payments over time.

Buyers and sellers should not confuse the value of the business with how the buyer finances the purchase, although they are inter-related. Consider two transactions. One, where the seller is willing to entertain an offer with a small down payment and to be paid the balance over a number of years, with a second offer where the buyer is willing to offer a larger down payment and a much shorter payment period. The seller accepting the longer payment period would likely expect the practice to have a higher purchase price, or at least pay interest.

TIP *The earn-out period should not last longer than three years, unless there are tax reasons for extending it.*

While some buyers have the personal resources to pay for the practice, most transactions between individual advisors happen because the seller offers to take back a loan.

Other transactions have been financed through:

- traditional lenders, where the loan is secured by the assets and future income of the business, or a personal guarantee
- the buyer's firm, on a selected basis, to some advisors who are acquiring client assets from others who also work for the firm, or to advisors joining the firm primarily to transfer their practice to another advisor there.

TIP *The seller's role is critical to a successful transition. Most buyers want to structure the deal to ensure the seller will fulfill their role during the transition period. Some ideas include holding back some of the purchase price and/or building a retention bonus into the deal.*

KEY FINANCING FACTORS

Key financing factors include:

- the time value of money. A dollar paid today is worth more to the seller than a dollar paid in 24 months
- the size of the down payment
- the size of the loan and how long before it is paid off
- the investment risk
- the interest rate that reflects the risk inherent in the loan
- the opportunity cost of tying up the capital.

A buyer might compare the potential return of investing in a well-diversified portfolio with investing in, and operating, a financial planning practice.

SAMPLE PROMISSORY NOTE

CANADIAN DOLLARS $250,000.00.

WHEREAS the undersigned, Ann Black, has entered into an Agreement (the "Purchase Agreement") with Thomas Green, dated (date) with respect to the acquisition by the undersigned from Thomas Green of his Client Assets.

FOR VALUE RECEIVED AND SUBJECT TO THE TERMS AND CONDITIONS AS SET OUT IN THE SAID PURCHASE AGREEMENT, the undersigned hereby promises to pay to or to the order of Thomas Green at Toronto, Ontario, the Portfolio Purchase Price (as herein defined) as calculated and determined in accordance with section 3.02 of the Purchase Agreement and in such instalments and on such dates as are set forth in section 3.02 of the Purchase Agreement:

1. On account of the Portfolio Purchase Price, Purchaser shall pay $250,000.00 plus 50% of applicable GST thereon, as follows:
    a) $50,000.00 plus GST upon execution hereon
    b) the balance plus GST in equal payments on the last day of the ten subsequent quarters.
    c) any final adjustments on (Date).

This promissory note is not assignable without prior written consent of the other party and is to be construed in all respects and enforced in accordance with the laws of Ontario.

This Promissory Note shall bind the undersigned and her heirs, executors, administrators and assigns and shall endure to the benefit of Thomas Green and his heirs, executors, administrators, successors and assigns.

DATED this 13th day of (Date).

Ann Black

VENDOR-TAKE-BACK FINANCING (OR EARN-OUT)

The buyer may offer a down payment and ask the seller to extend vendor-take-back financing. The seller needs to determine if they are willing to extend credit to any potential buyer.

Where the seller is willing to provide vendor-take-back financing, the buyer will be asked to sign a personal promissory note, promising to make payments over a set period of time, with interim or final adjustments, according to the terms of the agreement.

The buyer may want to tie the payment dates to fall after the dates the quarterly service or trailer fees are normally paid. However, there could be a mismatch the revenues received and the payment required. The buyer should ensure that they have the financial resources to:

- make the payments as they come due
- pay the expenses of the business
- cover their living expenses until they can earn income from business.

If the price is determined upfront and the payment schedule is long, the buyer can normally be expected to pay the seller the going rate for a traditional loan, or two to three percent higher to reflect the associated risk. If the payment schedule is less than twelve months, the buyer might negotiate for an interest-free loan.

Where the price for the business is not determined upfront but is being paid according to a formula based on the actual client revenues received after the transaction date, the payments may be linked to those revenues.

Size Of The Down Payment

Most sellers expect to receive 25 to 50 percent of the anticipated purchase price as a down payment, with the balance paid over time. The larger the down payment, the stronger the implied buyer's commitment to make the most of the client list they are acquiring. Sometimes a seller will consider a lower-priced offer if it comes with a large down payment—as less money is at risk.

Risk Of Default

A seller who offers vendor-take-back financing assumes the risk as a creditor and the risk that the buyer could default, or become unable to run the business due to disability or death.

To protect the seller in the event the buyer defaults due to death, the seller may require the buyer to be insured under a policy owned by the seller for an amount equal to amount potentially at risk. If the buyer is uninsurable, the seller may require a larger down payment and a shorter payment schedule to reduce their risk.

The purchase and sale agreement may also have safeguards to help protect the seller in the event of default that might:

- require the buyer to pay the loan immediately in full
- revert the business back to the selling advisor.

The last thing most sellers would want to have to do is resume their role as an advisor, in the event the buyer defaults. Another alternative might be to sell the business to another buyer, but by then it might be only a shadow of its former state, and much less valuable.

The buyer should also ensure he or she can cover the loan payments in the event of disability before the loan is repaid.

THE TRADITIONAL LENDER

Although some traditional lenders may be willing to extend a business loan for a business which is primarily insurance-based, most traditional lenders are not interested in extending a loan that would be secured against the revenues from an investment-based business because:

- the income is more variable
- the business interest is difficult to assess
- it may not be able to use it as collateral.

However, they may be willing to provide the buyer with a loan that is personally guaranteed by the buyer or is secured against personal assets, such as their home.

TIP *Buyers who want the freedom to make all the decisions re-lated to the management and day-to-day operation of the business should ensure the financing terms do not require them to assign the lender an interest in the business.*

YOUR FIRM

Some dealer firms with strong balance sheets are willing to extend loans at competitive terms to some of their advisors (particularly senior or top advisors). Some insurance compa-nies also offer loan arrangements to planners and advisors who meet certain criteria.

STOCK OR STOCK OPTIONS

Strategic buyers often offer more than cash – they might in-clude stock options or shares to sweeten the deal.

If the seller's company is offering stock or stock options as part of the transaction, assess their value by considering:
- whether or not the stock is liquid.
- the shareholder value today. For example, is the company good enough that you might recommend its stock to your client portfolios (assuming there were no conflicts of inter-est)? Or is not suitable given its level of risk?
- whether or not the company is closely held. If it is closely held, does it have potential value if the business goes pub-lic?
- is the stock restricted or unrestricted? How long would they be held in escrow?
- is it a benefit today, or a potential benefit that ties you in to the firm?
- are you required to reach certain performance targets as part of the terms of the offer?

- is the firm interested in:
  - buying your business (with you still managing it) or
  - your client assets (with you being phased out)?

HOW DO YOU WANT TO PAY?

Preferred method(s) for financing the purchase (check all that apply)

❑ All cash

❑ Cash deposit of __% of purchase price

❑ Earn-out over __ months

❑ Vendor-take-back financing over __ months

❑ Private financing

❑ Firm financing

❑ Traditional financing

❑ Stock or stock options

❑ Negotiable

SUMMARY

Financing can be a hurdle to any deal. But once it is in place, the real work begins to finalize the deal and plan the transition.

⑧ FINALIZING THE DEAL

"In my mind, talent plus knowledge,
plus effort account for success."
Gertrude Samuels

The buyer and the seller have found each other. The buyer is completing the due diligence work and likes what they see. You've settled on a formula to use to establish the purchase price. There are just a few details—terms—to iron out before the deal is finalized. You're almost there.

NEGOTIATING THE TERMS OF THE DEAL

Negotiating the details is about finding the right balance between:
- paying the seller for the business they are selling
- the buyer paying for the client assets they actually receive.

As with any negotiations, each party needs to be clear regarding those issues they are willing to negotiate and where they need to stand firm. They need to be reasonable as they work out the remaining details and through the transition—and stay cool when their words are turned into legalese.

One rule of thumb when negotiating is to put a dollar value on what you would like to have happen, or the cost to you if something does not happen. For example, if it's important to the buyer that the seller personally introduce all key accounts to them as soon as possible, the buyer might want to tie a bonus payment to the completion of that activity.

Sometimes an independent third party can offer the buyer and seller an objective perspective for some of the more complex issues related to the terms of the sale.

 When only a few terms of the deal are stumbling blocks, some parties decide to split the terms down the middle — as long as neither party loses more than the other by doing so.

Here are some key points to consider during the negotiations that we have not yet discussed.

The Seller's Staff

If the buyer is interested in hiring some or all of the seller's staff, is he or she also willing to assume the liability for any future severance payments that would include their employment with the seller? You also need to consider if the compensation these employees receive from the seller is comparable to the compensation you offer.

 Consider paying the seller's key employees a retention bonus, particularly during the transition period, if you can do it in a way that would be fair to your current employees.

The Prospect List

The older the names and addresses are in any prospect list, the less valuable it is.

However, if the prospect list is active and has been developed according to specific criteria, it may be of some value to a buyer.

The seller could attach a price to it, or hold it back and use it as a small incentive at a key time in the negotiations.

Bringing In New Clients

The buyer could agree to pay the seller under a marketing agreement for marketing ideas that result in new business, provided this does not contravene any industry rules.

Transfer Fees

Where the assets are transferring from the seller's firm to the buyer's, who will be responsible for any transfer-out fees the relinquishing firm might charge for registered accounts and open investment accounts? Sometimes the acquiring firm will cover the cost; otherwise the buyer and the seller have to work out this detail.

Minimizing The Tax

As a financial advisor or planner, you pay attention to the tax implications of your clients' financial decisions. As a buyer or a seller, you'll want to pay attention to the tax implications of your transaction. Generally, sellers want to structure the transaction to minimize the tax consequences of the sale; buyers want to deduct the costs related to buying the business as quickly as possible. As a rule of thumb, the tax department expects there to be a match between the timing of the deductions made by the buyer and the income reported by the seller.

This section is a general discussion of some of the tax planning issues related to the client assets and the seller's goodwill. If real estate or depreciating assets such as computer equipment and furniture are involved, some advisors and planners may want to sell those assets under a separate agreement (even if they are sold to the same buyer) to maximize any related tax-planning opportunities.

DURING NEGOTIATIONS

The Seller	The Buyer
Wants to report proceeds from the sale as capital gains where possible, or over as many years as possible	Wants to deduct costs as quickly as possible to to minimize tax
Assumes revenues will go up	Assumes revenues will stay stable or shrink due to attrition

---

The structure of the practice or business is the starting point for tax planning.

Commissioned Employees

A commissioned employee is not considered to have a business that would qualify for preferred tax treatment. Income from a sale is generally taxed as regular income in the year it is received. Sellers who are commissioned employees might consider structuring part of the deal as a purchase and another part as a management or consulting contract to defer some of the income to the year in which the services are performed.

Incorporated Advisors and Planners

Many financial advisory and planning practices are built primarily with sweat equity. When incorporated practices are sold, they attract taxable capital gains and goodwill.

In Canada, when you sell the shares of a business for more than their adjusted cost base (ACB), income tax is due on that portion of the capital gains that must be included as taxable income (currently 50 percent of the profits).

For a qualified small business corporation, an enhanced capital gains exemption of up to $500,000 per shareholder may be available for capital gains triggered on the sale of shares if, generally speaking, it has not been held by anyone else in the 24 months immediately proceeding the transaction and which can pass two tests at the time of sale:

- 90 percent or more of its assets were used directly in an active business carried on in Canada
- in the prior 24 months, at least 50 percent of the corporate assets of were used principally in the active business.

The seller with a corporation may be able to claim a tax reserve equal to the amount financed, and spread the tax bill over up to five years by matching the tax on the income from the sale with the year that income is actually received.

Owners of incorporated businesses may also be able to minimize their taxes over the long term by setting up a family trust or triggering an estate freeze.

TIP *Obtain advice on how best to structure your transaction from an independent tax advisor, such as an accountant, business valuator or CPA, who will stand-by their opinion. Some tax planning strategies are not black-and-white.*

Other Taxes

Some transactions may also be subject to provincial or state taxes. For example, in Canada, some individuals performing services under a consulting or management contract may be required to collect the Goods and Services Tax (GST) or Harmonized Sales Tax (HST).

Work In Progress

If the business has any work in progress prior to the closing date, such as commissions earned but not paid, or hourly fees for work in progress, the buyer will want to be paid for all work done up to the closing date.

As well, if the seller can identify pending sales, they could be factored into the final sale price, provided they materialize within the specified period of time.

CALLING IN THE PROFESSIONALS

As the buyer and seller work through the process and informally agree on the basics for the agreement, each party should seek out independent business, legal and tax advice. Buying and selling a business is not a do-it-yourself project.

The right advisor can assist you in assessing the opportunity and refining the details and terms of the transaction. Through the transaction, they could act as a good sounding board and, in the final stages of the transaction, act as a mediator/negotiator on your behalf.

These professionals might include:

- a lawyer to draw up the legally binding agreements.
- an accountant to help with the tax implications of the transaction
- a chartered business valuator holding the CBV designation who can help value book of business and non-client assets
- a banker who could assist in arranging a personal or business loan, or a line of credit to a qualified buyer so they have enough cash flow to run the business, in the event it does not produce enough income in the short term
- a business consultant or broker who understands this business.

Your professional advisors should tell you what you need to hear, not just what you want to hear. They might even recommend walking away from a transaction that would not in your best interest.

Most professionals base their fees on the number of hours required, regardless of whether or not the transaction is completed, although some business brokers are paid a percentage of the purchase price when the transaction closes (if it closes). The buyer and seller normally pay for their own advisors.

THE PAPERWORK

Once the buyer has completed the due diligence work and negotiated the deal, the formal paperwork has to be drawn up and signed.

Each transaction is slightly different and your lawyers will provide wording that is appropriate to your deal and the province or state where you are located.

Here are some of the key ideas that might be included in the formal paperwork.

Non-Compete Agreement

While the value of non-compete agreements can be debated, the overall purpose is to protect the buyer by prohibiting the seller from competing or soliciting, directly or indirectly, with the buyer for the business from the existing clients, or anyone living at the same address as the client. A seller competing with the buyer for clients would undermine the intention of the deal — to sell the practice as a going concern.

> **TIP**   *In addition to the seller signing the non-compete or non-solicitation agreement, the buyer may want the seller's key staff and/or his or her spouse to also sign agreements that they will not solicit the seller's clients.*

The terms of the non-compete agreement should be reasonable and appropriate. If the terms are overly restrictive, the agreement may not be enforceable by the buyer.   The non-compete agreement should:
- reflect the need of the buyer to restrict the seller from soliciting the clients being sold
- be specific as to what would constitute competition, such as activities in the same geographic region
- not restrict the seller for longer than necessary

- provide a penalty clause stating how the seller will reimburse the buyer in the event the non-compete clause were violated.

SAMPLE NON-COMPETE AGREEMENT

WHEREAS Thomas Green, ABC Investment Inc., and Ann Black, The Great Canadian Financial Group have entered into an Agreement (the "Purchase Agreement") dated (Date), with respect to the acquisition by Ann Black from Thomas Green of his Client Assets.

FOR VALUE RECEIVED AND SUBJECT TO THE TERMS AND CONDITIONS AS SET OUT IN THE SAID PURCHASE AGREEMENT, Thomas Green hereby covenants and agrees as follows:

1. Thomas Green, individually or together or in conjunction with any other individual, partnership, association or corporation, SHALL NOT for a period of (Length) from the (Date), within the Province of Ontario provide, offer to provide, or solicit a request to provide any asset management, investment, insurance, and/or financial planning services whatsoever to any person, firm, association, corporation or other entity.

2. In the event of a breach of section 1 above, Thomas Green shall be indebted to Ann Black for damages in the amount which is equal to (formula for amount) as established by the parties and agrees to pay the said damages to Ann Black forthwith upon demand.

3. To the extent permitted by applicable law, if it is held that the provisions herein do not contain reasonable limitations as to time, scope or geographical area, then the courts may, as requested by Ann Black, reform such provisions to make them reasonable, and this covenant shall be deemed to be amended accordingly retroactively.

4. The parties agree to use their best efforts to resolve disputes by regarding this non-competition covenant by negotiation. In the event that a dispute occurs that cannot be resolved by negotiation between the parties, the parties agree to use the services of a mediator to attempt to resolve their differences.

    This clause does not preclude the parties from taking all necessary legal steps, including self-help remedies, or from taking steps to have their dispute resolved by any other appropriate dispute resolution process, including arbitration of the appropriate Court process.

However, each party covenants and agrees that litigation shall be the recourse of last resort and shall be utilized only when that party, acting reasonably, has determined that all other appropriate dispute resolution steps have not or will not be productive.

5. This Covenant shall be binding upon Thomas Green and his heirs, executors, administrators, successors and assigns, and endure to the benefit of Ann Black and her heirs, executors, administrators, successors and assigns.

IN WITNESS WHEREOF the undersigned has duly executed this covenant under his hand and seal of the (Date).

SIGNED, SEALED & DELIVERED

Thomas Green_____   Ann Black_____

For advisors who are selling only part of their book of client assets, a non-solicitation agreement might be more appropriate. In a non-solicitation agreement, the seller would agree not to solicit those clients for a specified period of time.

 To avoid costly legal fees in the event a non-compete clause were breached, consider including a buyout clause in the purchase agreement where the seller would reimburse the buyer in the event that a client did leave to join the seller or the seller's new firm. As a deterrent the clause might require the seller to reimburse the buyer for as much as double the original purchase (related to that client).

Purchase And Sale Agreement

After the potential buyer has looked at the business and performed their due diligence, they will have their lawyer draw up a Purchase and Sale Agreement. Unlike the offer to purchase a home, there is no standard form that is used for the purchase and sale of a financial advisory practice.

The seller should then take the unsigned Purchase and Sale Agreement and any other paperwork related to the agreement to their own lawyer to make sure their legal rights and interests are protected. The seller's lawyer may make suggestions for changes and the agreement could go back and forth a few times before the buyer and seller both agree on its content. Some of the clauses they add to protect the seller or the buyer may cause strain on the negotiations. It can help to consider a number of scenarios, including good and not so good, so that the interests of each party are protected.

In the appendix, I've included a sample purchase and sale agreement with some of the types of clauses that could be included in an agreement. However, every agreement will be personalized to document the agreement between the buyer and the seller.

Once the terms of the Purchase and Sale Agreement have been negotiated and signed off, the offer is final, even if the price is not. If the final price is not firm, the agreement will have established how it is be calculated.

The following are some of the clauses that should be considered for a purchase and sale agreement, as well as some points to consider:

- definitions of terms used in the agreement
- the terms and conditions of the offer to purchase, including the price
- what is being sold, the list of client assets or shares of a business
- retention factors that would increase or decrease the price
- the price for other assets, such as real estate or software
- a release from all obligations of the seller
- the transition plan
- services provided by the seller during the transition period
- who is responsible for staff salaries and expenses related to transition
- closing dates
- the warranties and guarantees of each party
- extent of liability
- how disputes will be resolved.

The Terms And Conditions Of The Offer

The terms of the offer to purchase include:
- the purchase price, or the formula to be used to determine the purchase price
- the size of the down payment
- any vendor-take-back financing.

If the offer is subject to any conditions, such as the buyer being able to obtain financing, any regulatory approval required, or being approved by the firm as a new hire, they would also be documented.

The Client Assets

The assets may be the client assets or the shares of a business.

A list of client may be attached to the purchase and sale agreement. The list would include the client names, account numbers, and depending on the basis for the purchase price, the value of assets under management, revenue by client and/or the financial statements of the business. This list could be used to identify the client assets for future adjustments or bonuses, as well as for any non-compete or non-solicitation agreement.

Adjustments Or Bonuses

As we discussed, some buyers do not want to pay for client assets that are not retained. If the buyer and seller agree to a retention bonus or adjustment to the purchase price based on assets retained, it would be included. See the chapter titled Factoring Attrition Into The Equation.

An agreement may contain a clause to protect the buyer's trailers in the event the buyer's code is not changed at the fund company on a timely basis. The clause might require the seller to pay the buyer the value of commissions and trailers that were earned by the buyer but paid directly to the seller after the transaction date.

Other Assets

All non-client assets, if any, being sold need to be documented in the purchase and sale agreement or in a separate agreement. In many transactions there is a broad range that some of these assets are sold for. Some sellers just want them taken off their hands; other sellers want to profit from them.

The Transition Plan

The transition plan and the roles and responsibilities of the buyer and the seller would be documented, including who is to do what and when.

Role Of Seller During Transition Period

In a professional service, the role of the seller during the transition period is crucial to the success of the transaction. The seller's efforts would be required primarily in the first few months of the transition period, gradually phasing out by six to twelve months.

A reasonable amount of seller's time would normally be included as part of the base purchase price. If the buyer expects the seller to remain active in the business and is therefore unable to move on to other things, the seller would expect to be compensated for their time, either directly for the time or through a higher selling price. You wouldn't work for free, would you?

Transition Salaries And Expenses

There are expenses and salaries to be paid during the transition. In some transactions, the buyer is responsible for the salaries and the transition expenses. In other transactions, the buyer is responsible for some and the buyer and the seller jointly responsible for other expenses.

When To Close

The best quarters to close the transaction are those ending:

- March 31 (unless you prepare tax returns)
- June 30
- September 30 if you can complete most of the transition work before year-end.

If you can, avoid December 31.

TIP *Pick closing date(s) that matches a date on which most third-party suppliers provide reports, such as at the end of the quarter.*

Warranties And Guarantees Of Each Party

The buyer and the seller each warranty and guarantee a number of items, including that:
- they both have the authority to enter into the transaction
- the seller will release to the buyer all information required to complete the transaction
- all statements made have been true
- this agreement does not breach any other agreements the parties have with others, such as a buy-sell agreement with someone else, or an agreement with their firm.

Extent Of Liability

The seller is normally liable for any errors or wrongdoings related to activities prior to the closing date, and the buyer for errors or wrongdoings that can be traced to their own actions or advice, except when the buyer and the seller are sharing commissions or jointly advising the client.

Dispute Resolution

It makes sense in many transactions, for the buyer and the seller to agree to use their best efforts to resolve any disputes that may occur by negotiation, mediation, or arbitration to avoid going to court, if at all possible.

MANAGEMENT CONSULTING CONTRACTS OR SERVICE AGREEMENTS

The buyer may expect the seller to be available for some consultation through the transition period and perhaps beyond. If the buyer anticipates they might need the seller to be available for longer than what might be considered a reasonable amount of time to assist with the transition, he or she may want to offer the seller a management consulting agreement or service agreement.

These agreements could be included as part of the purchase and sale agreement, or in a separate agreement. Compensation of the seller's time could be:

- negotiated as part of the purchase and sale agreement and factored into the purchase price
- paid on a pay-as-you-go basis at a specified hourly rate for the seller's post-sale services
- a combination .

TIP *If the seller gives up their licences, they will not be able to provide clients with investment advice on an ongoing basis or to split commissions.*

SUMMARY

Once the agreements are signed, the work begins to transition the clients from the buyer to the seller.

⑨
THE TRANSITION PLAN

"Success usually comes to those who
are too busy to be looking for it."
Henry David Thoreau

The buyer and seller have worked through the details of the transaction and the deal looks like it is going to happen. Now the buyer and the seller have to plan the transition to minimize client attrition and maximize its success. In fact, they should be planning the transition before the final price is set and the transaction is closed.

Transition includes everything from preparing your business for the transaction, introducing the new advisor to the clients, and the buyer and seller working together in some manner for a period of time. The due diligence will have given the buyer a good idea of the strengths and weaknesses of the business—and time to think through ways to integrate the new clients into their existing practice.

There are many different ways to structure an effective transition, but the most successful ones retain clients and their assets, establish ongoing relationships with those clients and maintain (or increase) the profits earned from these clients. The transition plan should include:

- a client communication plan outlining why it is in their best interests to work with the successor advisor

- working with staff to address their concerns, which may include "will they have a job?" and "how will we do all the added work?"
- quickly setting up client meetings so they can meet one-on-one with the successor advisor.

TIP *Don't announce the deal until all the paperwork is signed and the down payment paid.*

If the transaction is between two people at the same firm, your firm may already have some procedures in place that could help you work through the transition. If the transaction is between people at different firms, the buyer's firm may have a team that could help with the transition, otherwise the buyer may need to hire temporary staff to assist with the paperwork required.

Buyers need to prepare their existing business so it has the capacity and systems in place to deal with the seller's clients.

TIP *Prior to the transaction date, buyers should accelerate their service schedule for their existing clients to free up some time to focus on integrating the new clients.*

THE INTRODUCTIONS

Introduce The Buyer To The Seller's Clients

The seller will be required to introduce the buyer to the clients. This introduction could include:

1. a joint event, such as an evening workshop or reception, where the clients are introduced to the new advisor and their team
2. a referral letter signed by the seller informing the clients of the imminent change and introducing the buyer and their expertise
3. phone call from the buyer following up the referral letter
4. a personal call from seller where appropriate

5. client meetings attended by both the buyer and the seller, as required.

The buyer and the seller will have to assess the individual client needs to determine if the buyer and the seller should meet jointly with selected clients, or all the clients in the book.

TIP *When the transaction involves only some of the seller's clients, determine how to tell them why some clients are changing advisors and not others.*

When I sold my practice, the buyer and I hosted an evening cocktail event that was also attended by the company president. Everyone made a brief speech. I spoke about the upcoming changes to my practice and introduced my successor, who spoke briefly about her investment philosophy and commitment to clients, and her team. The president discussed the direction of the company and invited the clients to call him directly with any questions or concerns. The evening had a warm feeling and provided the clients with a firsthand look at what we were doing, and the confidence that we would be supporting each other. While not all clients could or were interested in attending, word spread that the evening was a success.

Those clients who had been invited to the seminar but could not attend received a follow-up letter summarizing the evening's events, and inviting them to call either myself or the buyer directly. Over a 10-day period, clients who had not been invited to the event received a version of the letter that did not mention it. Within two days of mailing these letters, the buyer called each client personally to set up an initial meeting.

Given the size of the client base, we had originally planned to tell the top one-third of clients first, then the next third, and then the rest. However, after I considered the web of my client network, I felt it was necessary to tell all clients at the same time. Even though this required intense work over a shorter period of time, we both felt it would be better for clients to hear the news from us, rather than one of their friends.

TIP *Prepare scripts for buyer, seller and their staff to use so that clients receive a consistent message regarding the transaction, no matter who they speak to.*

If the seller is able to position the transfer of client assets as a succession plan, rather than a sale, and can wholeheartedly refer the clients to the new advisor, it will increase the retention rate. Clients don't like to think they've been "sold."

TIP *Provide the clients with some continuity to their previous advisor, where possible. Perhaps the seller could attend on-going events as a special guest or write a guest column in the buyer's newsletter.*

Introduce The Clients To The Buyer's Staff

It's also important to introduce the buyer's staff to the seller's clients, and if the buyer is retaining any of the seller's staff, to introduce them to the buyer's clients.

This could be done:

- at any event held
- in written correspondence
- in the office.

Take the time to introduce clients to the team when they come to the office for any reason.

Any staff whose services will not be required by the buyer after the transaction date would be given adequate notice and the value of their termination package calculated.

TIP *To help clients appreciate that the buyer is there to help them reach their financial goals, the buyer's team could remind clients who call in that you are in the office by asking the client if they "would like you to call." This reinforces that the new advisor is there for them.*

Introduce The Buyer To The Seller's Centre Of Influences

If a number of the seller's clients were originally referred by the seller's centre of influence network or as a result of a strategic alliance, those client relationships could be at risk.

It is important for the seller to introduce the buyer to those COI and strategic alliances to communicate:
- the experience and expertise of the buyer
- how the relationship will continue.

Introduce The Transaction To The Buyer's Existing Clients

The buyer's existing client base will hear about the deal, one way or another. It can be important for the buyer to reassure those clients that they will continue to have time for them.

TIP *The buyer can build some capacity to process the new client paperwork by hiring temporary qualified help, working with the seller for a period of time and ensuring the needs of the existing clients are up-to-date.*

THE CLIENT MEETINGS

One-On-One Meetings With The Clients

While buying a book of client assets may be the ultimate referral, there is a ton of initial work to convert the selling advisor's client base into the buyer's own loyal clients.

TIP *To help the buyer prepare for the first client meeting, the seller should review the client history and the client's situation with them.*

While some buyers want the seller to attend all the initial client meetings, others prefer to start to build the one-on-one relationship with the client from the very first meeting, particularly when the buyer and seller have already held a joint event.

Consider how many one-on-one meetings it could take before the client considers him or herself to be the successor's client. While they may sign the necessary paperwork in the first meeting so transactions can be processed on their behalf, this is not enough for the buyer to establish a working relationship with them. As with any prospect, expect to have to meet with them two or three times before they become long-term client.

TIP *Some transition periods operate as a partnership between the buyer and the seller to give the clients time to get to know the buyer.*

Be prepared to meet with each client up to three times within the first six months of the deal closing to introduce yourself and your services, answer any questions the client has, get to know the client and their needs, and explain any processes, reports or statements you provide. It is also helpful to take a financial planning approach to working with these clients. Although it is time-consuming, it helps the client feel you understand their needs.

You could have difficulty keeping all the new client names, faces and circumstances straight without referring to their files and your notes. If you haven't before, you'd better learn to take good notes!

Some agreements have been structured to phase the selling advisor's clients into the buyer's practice and give the buyer the time to meet and process all the required client paperwork. For example, one-third of the clients might be transferred in the spring, one-third in the summer and the final third in the fall.

HOW MANY MEETINGS WILL YOU HAVE?

Suppose you are buying a business with 200 client families. You plan to meet with the top 100 families three times, the next 50 families two times and the remaining families once each.

Meetings Required	Number of Client Families	Total Meetings
3	100	300
2	50	100
1	50	50
		450

That's about 450 meetings within six months—over and above the meetings you'll have with your existing clients! You need to consider how many new clients you can physically handle. What you want to do and what you can physically do may not be the same.

THE ADMINISTRATION

Complete The Paperwork To Transfer The Client Accounts

Client paperwork

Forms will have to be prepared for the new client's signature. This paperwork would include an updated Client Application form (or the know-your-client information) and the forms required to transfer the client accounts to the buyer's production code.

> **TIP** *To deal with issues related to the confidentiality of the client information, have the client sign a release form authorizing the seller to release their information to the buyer.*

For compliance reasons, it may not be possible to move the original client file from one firm to another firm, even if the firm of the selling advisor accepts the transaction.

The seller should contact existing product suppliers, including mutual fund companies and insurers to authorize the client assets be transferred to the buyer and to anticipate the paperwork.

Block transfers

If you are able to arrange for a block or bulk transfer of the clients' assets from the selling advisor to the buying advisor, you may not have to get written consent from each and every client to transfer their account. Your compliance officer will confirm if this is an option.

TIP *It takes time to re-register assets. If you read the product providers' fine print, you'll find that some state that the trailer fees are paid when the assets have been held for the full period (i.e. the full month or full quarter). This rule could affect both the buyer and the seller negatively if the date of the transition is not well-thought-out. Contact your product representative or wholesaler for clarification of how these rules would affect you.*

Train The Buyer And Their Staff On Procedures And Systems

If required, the seller and/or a member of their team will need to train the buyer and/or their team on certain procedures they use with the clients, and/or any systems that buyer is acquiring.

Seller To Provide Buyer With Sample Form Letters, Newsletters, Statements And Reports Used

The buyer will likely want to receive sample form letters, newsletter templates, statements and reports so they know what the clients are used to receiving. While they may or may not use these with their existing clients or even the clients they acquire, they need this information so they can explain the differences to the clients, if necessary.

Seller To Provide Buyer With Client Word Processing And Spreadsheet Files

Converting from paper files to an automated system is labour-intensive. If the seller can provide the buyer with the electronic word processing and spreadsheet files, they could import the data into their programs.

Make Sure All Accounts Transfer To The Buyer

The buyer will not be paid for the client assets unless they are registered as the advisor on record. The buyer needs to track the investments to make sure their code(s) are changed on at timely basis at the manufacturer level. For internal transactions (between financial advisors who work at the same firm), just changing the code on the corporate system is not enough

TIP *If it seems to be taking a long time to get the accounts transferred, even when all the paperwork has been completed properly, consider asking a few of your clients to voice their complaint.*

Seller's Housekeeping

If the seller is leaving the business, they may also need to:
- return any company materials under the terms of employment
- prepare a letter of resignation
- submit the required paperwork to securities regulators
- advise professional associations of change of status or address
- terminate applicable leases
- provide staff with a letter of reference.

SUMMARY

Planning the transition can help the buyer manage the effort that is required.

KEYS TO SUCCESS

"The three great essentials to achieve anything
worth while are, first, hard work; second,
stick-to-itiveness; third, common-sense."
Thomas Edison

A successful transaction is one where everyone involved wins, the seller, the buyer, the firm they work for and the clients they serve. For this to happen:

- the price needs to be fair to both the buyer and the seller
- the buyer and seller have to work towards the common goal of retaining the assets
- the clients must see the change as the seller's succession plan, rather than a purchase/sale arrangement.

Eventually, we all leave the business, on account of retirement, career change, disability or death. Among the advisors over 55 who participated in the 2001 Financial Advice in Canada study, 47 percent indicated they were planning to retire in one to five years, 24 percent in six to 10 years and 29 percent not for more than 10 years.

For buyers, the opportunity to grow your assets under management and your profits by purchasing a book of business is exciting. In fact, the seller's endorsement of the buyer may be the ultimate referral in this business. But it is important to carefully assess the opportunity you may have and determine if it is a business or a book of business? This requires careful assessment of the practice, its potential and the compatibility of the clients and their assets.

Since a practice is valued primarily on the revenue and profits that it earns, the seller should work to keep their profits and revenues stable or growing. Practices with declining revenues or no profits are not as attractive to potential buyers.

ADVISORS PLANNING TO RETIRE IN SIX TO 10 YEARS

How old are the advisors who indicated they were planning to retire in six to 10 years?

Age	Percentage
Under 30	2%
31-40	7%
41-50	36%
51-55	44%
55+	11%

Source: Headspring Consulting Inc.
2001 Financial Advice in Canada Study

If you are considering an exit strategy within the next five years, now would be a good time to evaluate your practice — a potential buyer will want to know how the business is really doing — and take steps to protect and maximize its value. But don't sell before you are ready. Working for a few more years might generate as much income as you might get from selling your practice.

If you are not planning on exiting the business in the next few years, you owe it to yourself to protect the value of your business by having a formal exit strategy in the event of death or disability — the final "sale." Without adequate planning, the value of your business on death could shrink — attrition would be higher because you would not be there to assist with the transition or endorse your successor.

Your long-term exit strategy could include:

- hiring a junior associate with the view to having them acquire your client base over time
- entering into a buy/sell agreement with another advisor at your firm or a new partner
- pre-selling your practice to your firm.

Although many financial advisors and planners recommend buy-sell agreement to their business owner clients, they often do not have one to protect their own business.

Throughout this book, we've considered many issues related to buying and selling a financial advisory or planning practice. Here are seven keys to a successful transaction.

SEVEN KEYS TO SUCCESS

1. Positioning the deal as a succession plan rather than a sale
2. Personal endorsement of the buyer by the seller
3. Participation by the buyer and seller during transition
4. Paperwork prepared by independent legal and tax advisors
5. Preparation in anticipation of the transaction
6. The right price
7. Perspiration—from old-fashioned hard work.

Sellers may find it difficult to leave the clients they have spent years serving. I did, and then it finally hit me. After one client family moved to BC and another died, I came to the conclusion that my job was to provide the best advice and service to my clients, but it wasn't necessarily a relationship that was until "death do us part." When it's time to move on, the seller's last job (subject to their agreement with their firm) is to find a successor for your business.

"Your legacy will ultimately be a manifestation of the deepest and the best...person you now are and the person you aim to be. Leaving a legacy is not about impressing your friends or reaching the top. It is not about looking good but about doing good. It's about fulfilling your duty and actualizing your humanity."

The Monk Who Sold His Ferrari

APPENDIX

SAMPLE PURCHASE AND SALE AGREEMENT

The following sample purchase and sale agreement is included here to illustrate some of the clauses that a lawyer might include in documents formalizing the purchase and sale of a financial advisory or planning practice. The purchase and sale agreement will be tailored to the laws of your jurisdiction, the nature of your business, the assets that you are selling and more.

Note: This sample agreement, and the other samples in the book, are not complete and should not be used to draw up your own documents.

---

*For Illustration Purposes Only

SAMPLE PURCHASE AGREEMENT

THIS AGREEMENT MADE THIS (Date)

BETWEEN:

> Thomas Green, of the City of Toronto (herein called the "Vendor")
> affiliated with ABC Investment Inc. (herein called "ABC")

AND:

> Ann Black, of the City of Toronto (herein called the "Purchaser")
> affiliated with The Great Canadian Financial Group (GCFC)
> (herein called "GCFC")

1.0 RECITALS

1.01 Vendor is a mutual fund salesperson affiliated with ABC Investments. Purchaser is a salesperson affiliated with GCFC.

1.02 Vendor wishes to transfer to Purchaser, and Purchaser wishes to acquire from Vendor, the Vendor's benefits, rights and entitlements in respect to Vendor's Client Assets.

THE PARTIES AGREE AS FOLLOWS:

2.0 INTERPRETATION

2.01 Definitions

In this Agreement hereto, unless there is something in the subject matter or context inconsistent therewith, the following terms and expressions will have the following meanings:

a) "Client" means any person for whcm financial assets are being held as at the close of business (Date), by Vendor, as that Client's licensed sales representative, through ABC Investment Inc., or other institution and any spouse, child, grandchild or parent cohabiting with such Client as at the close of business on (Date) and subsequent heir of such persons.

b) "Client Asset Accounts" means the financial assets of a Client, including, but not limited to, mutual funds, bonds, investment certificates, term deposits, mortgages, education savings plans, retirement savings plans, retirement income funds, stocks, limited partnership assets and insurance products as of (Date), but excludes financial assets in respect of which, on or before the close of business (Date), any Client had communicated to Vendor his intention to terminate.

c) "Encumbrances" means mortgages, charges, pledges, security interests, encumbrances, actions, claims, demands and equities of any nature.

d) "Person" means any individual, corporation, partnership, firm, joint venture, syndicate, association and trust.

e) "Portfolio Purchase Price" means the consideration payable to Vendor pursuant to section 3.02.

f) "Client Assets" means all Client Asset Accounts and includes Vendor's client lists, files, records, goodwill, benefits, rights and entitlements in respect thereto.

g) "Portfolio Value" means the value of the Portfolio as at a specified date, as verified to Purchaser's satisfaction, acting reasonably, by ABC Investment Inc.

2.02 Choice of Law and Attornment

This Agreement shall be construed in accordance with the laws of the Province of Ontario and Canada applicable herein. The parties agree that the courts of the Province of Ontario will have exclusive jurisdiction.

2.03 Independent Legal Counsel
The parties acknowledge that their respective legal counsel have reviewed and participated in settling the terms of this Agreement. The parties agree that any rule of construction stipulating that any ambiguity is to be resolved against the drafting party shall not be applicable in the interpretation of this Agreement.

3.0 PORTFOLIO PURCHASE AND SALE, CONSIDERATION AND RELATED SERVICES

3.01 Portfolio Purchase and Sale
Vendor agrees to sell, and Purchaser agrees to purchase, the Portfolio as hereinafter provided.

3.02 Consideration for Portfolio Purchase Price
On account of Portfolio Purchase Price, Purchaser agrees to pay Vendor Consideration equal to 0.5% of the Portfolio Value as at the close of business on (Date), as agreed upon by the parties in writing by (Date), subject to potential reduction thereafter pursuant to sections 2.01 (b) but not otherwise, plus GST thereon, if any.

The Consideration shall be allocated and paid as follows:
On account of the Portfolio Purchase Price, Purchaser shall pay $250,000.00 as follows:
$50,000.00 plus GST thereon, upon execution hereon
The balance plus GST on the last day of the eight subsequent quarters in equal amounts.
Any the final adjustments on (Date).
Upon execution hereof, Purchaser shall provide the Vendor with a promissory note for the fees.

3.03 GST
The Purchaser acknowledges that they will be responsible for the Goods and Services Tax, in addition to the Portfolio Purchase Price.

Each party hereby, indemnifies and holds each other harmless with respect to their respective obligation for Harmonized Services Tax as herein required.

4.0 REPRESENTATIONS AND WARRANTIES

4.01 Representations and Warranties by Vendor
Vendor represents and warrants to Purchaser as follows, same to survive completion of the transactions contemplated herein:

a)   Vendor has good right, power and authority to enter into this Agreement.

b)   No person, other than Purchaser, has any agreement or right to purchase the Client Assets.

c)   The books and records of Vendor in respect to the Portfolio are true, correct and complete in all materials respects and fairly present the Client Assets.

d)   There are no actions or proceedings, pending or threatened, affecting the Portfolio or the Vendor.

e)   The Portfolio is free and clear of Encumbrances, save and except for splits of commissions, trailers and/or other like compensation, of which Vendor shall have advised Purchaser in writing on or before execution of the Agreement.

f)   No statement, representation or warranty on the part of Vendor or in any schedule, certificate, list, summary or other disclosure document provided or to be provided to Purchaser contains or will contain any untrue statement of material fact, or omits or will omit to state any material fact necessary to make the statements contained therein not misleading.

4.02 Representations and Warranties by Purchaser

Purchaser hereby represents and warrants to Vendor as follows, same to survive completion of the transactions contemplated herein:

a)   Purchaser has good right, power and authority to enter into this Agreement.

b)   Purchaser is not under any obligation to request or obtain any consent, other than of a Client, to validly sell the Client Assets.

5.0 SERVICES: COVENANTS OF VENDOR AND PURCHASER

5.01 Services To Be Provided By The Vendor

From the execution hereof to (Date), inclusive, the Vendor, at all material times, as requested by Purchaser acting reasonably and in good faith, make available, without substitution, to do the following:

a)   Provide Purchaser with full particulars of and access to, the assets and records of the Client Asset Accounts pending receipt by Vendor from each Client of written authorization designating Purchaser as its mutual fund representative and then to deliver up all such books and records to Purchaser.

b)   Deliver to Purchaser, on or before (Date), a true and complete list of all Clients and Client Asset Accounts as at the close of business on (Date).

c)   Consulting services at the rate of $100/hour as required.

d)   Use best efforts to cause all necessary steps and proceedings to be taken in order to duly and regularly transfer the Client Assets to Purchaser.

e)   Review all client files with Purchaser.

   f)   It is understood that Vendor makes no guarantee that the consent of Clients will be forthcoming in this regard.

   g)   Provide to Purchaser samples of any and all of Vendor's form letters.

   h)   Introduce Purchaser to each Client by letter, phone, fax or in person, as jointly determined by the parties, acting reasonably.

5.02 Covenants of Vendor

   a)   Vendor shall promptly advise Purchaser of any facts that would cause any of their representations and warranties herein to be untrue in any respect.

   b)   Vendor shall take all actions within their control to preserve the Portfolio for transfer to Purchaser.

   c)   Vendor shall promptly advise Purchaser in writing of any material adverse change in the Portfolio.

   d)   Vendor shall keep in full force all of Vendor's current professional liability insurance policies for such time for 24 months following the purchase date.

   e)   Vendor shall provide to Purchaser all paper and electronic files of Clients, including contact files, as Purchaser becomes designated as their registered representative.

   f)   Vendor will execute and deliver to Purchaser a non-competition covenant upon execution of the Agreement.

5.03 Covenants of Purchaser

   a)   Purchaser will keep confidential all information relating to the Portfolio save and except that same may be disclosed to Purchaser's assistants and advisors. If the transactions contemplated hereby are not consummated for any reason, Purchaser will return forthwith, without retaining any copies thereof, all information and documents obtained from Vendor.

   b)   Purchaser will use best efforts to complete all paperwork required in order to duly and regularly have the Portfolio transferred from Vendor to Purchaser and to become recorded as the registered representative of the Clients.

   c)   Purchaser will pay, in a timely fashion, that portion of the salary and benefits of the Vendor's assistant relating to the time devoted in training Purchaser and Purchaser's assistant(s).

   d)   Purchaser will keep in full force all professional liability insurance policies at all material times.

   e)   Purchaser will keep in full force all licences and/or registrations under the Securities Act (Ontario) required to professionally service the Portfolio.

6.0 INDEMNIFICATION AND SET-OFF

6.01 Indemnification by Vendor and Purchaser

a) Vendor hereby indemnifies and saves Purchaser harmless from and against any damages, losses, costs, liabilities and expenses which may be suffered by Purchaser arising out of:

  (i) any non-performance or non-fulfillment of any covenant or agreement on their part contained herein or in any document given pursuant hereto;

  (ii) any misrepresentation, inaccuracy, incorrectness or breach of any representation or warranty made by them contained herein or in any document given pursuant hereto; and

  (iii) all cost and expenses including without limitation, legal fees on a solicitor-and-client basis, incidental to or in respect of the foregoing provided that the liability of Vendor hereunder shall be limited to the Portfolio Purchase Price.

b) Purchaser hereby indemnifies and saves Vendor harmless from and against any damages, losses, costs, liabilities and expenses which may be suffered by them arising out of:

  (i) any misrepresentation, inaccuracy, incorrectness or breach of any representation or warranty made by them contained herein or in any document given pursuant hereto; and

  (ii) all cost and expenses including without limitation, legal fees on a solicitor-and-client basis, incidental to or in respect of the foregoing; provided that the liability of Purchaser together hereunder shall be limited to the Portfolio Purchase Price.

7.0 GENERAL PROVISIONS

7.01 Further Assurances

Each of the parties hereby agree that after the execution of the Agreement, it will, upon request of any other, do, execute, acknowledge and deliver or agree to do, execute, acknowledge or deliver all such further acts, deeds, assignments, transfers, conveyances and assurances as may be required for the better carry out and performance of all the terms of this Agreement.

7.02 Any single or partial exercise by any party hereto of any fright or remedy for refusal or breach of any term, covenant or condition of this Agreement does not waive, alter, affect or prejudice any other right or remedy to which such party may be lawfully entitled for the same default or breach.

7.03 Notices

a) Any notice, designation, communication, request, demand, or other document, required or permitted to be given or sent or delivered hereunder to any party hereto shall be in writing and shall be sufficiently given, sent or delivered if it is:

  (i)   delivered personally to such party

  (ii)   sent to the party by registered mail, postage prepaid, mailed in Canada, or

  (iii)   sent by fax machine.

b)   Notices shall be sent to the following addresses or fax numbers:

  (i)   in the case of the Vendor, to 99 Blue Street, Toronto, Ontario M6G 7K9

  (ii)   in the case of the Purchaser, to 88 White Street, Toronto, Ontario M9C 5K6

  (iii)   Or to such other address or fax number as the party entitled to or receiving such notice, designation, communication, request, demand or other document shall, by a notice given in accordance with this section, have communicated to the party giving or sending or delivering such notice, designation, communication, request demand or other document.

c)   Any notice designation, communication, request, demand or other document given or sent or delivered as aforesaid shall:

  (i)   if delivered in person, be deemed to have been given, sent, delivered and received on the date of delivery

  (ii)   if sent by mail as above, be deemed to have been given, sent, delivered and received (but not actually received, on the fourth Business Day following the date of mailing, unless at any time between the date of mailing and the fourth Business Day unless there is a discontinuance or interruption of regular postal service, where duty to strike or lockout or work slowdown, affecting postal service at the point of dispatch or delivery or any intermediate point, in which case it will have been deemed to have been sent, delivered and received in the ordinary course of the mail, allowing for such discontinuance or interruption of regular postal service, and

  (iii)   if sent by fax machine, be deemed to have been given, sent, delivered and received on the date shown on the sender confirmation receipt.

7.04 Expenses of Parties

Each of the parties hereto shall bear all expenses incurred by it in connection with this Agreement including, without limitation, the charges of their respective counsel, accountants, and financial advisors.

7.05 Announcements

No announcement with respect to this Agreement will be made without the prior approval of all parties.

The foregoing will not apply to any announcement required in order to comply with laws pertaining to timely disclosure, provided that such party consults with the other parties before making any such announcement.

7.06 Assignment
The rights of Vendor hereunder shall not be assignable without the written consent of Purchaser. The rights of Purchaser hereunder shall not be assignable without the written consent of Vendor.

7.07 Successors and Assigns
This Agreement shall be binding upon and endure to the benefit of the parties hereto and their respective heirs, executors, administrators, successor and permitted assigns.

7.08 Dispute Resolution/Mediation
The parties agree to use their best efforts to resolve disputes by negotiation. In the event that a dispute occurs that cannot be resolved by negotiation, the parties agree to use the services of a mediator to attempt to resolve their differences. This clause does not preclude the parties from taking all necessary legal steps or from taking steps to have their dispute resolved by any other appropriate dispute resolution process, including arbitration or the appropriate Court process. However, each party covenants and agrees that litigation shall be the recourse of last resort and shall be utilized only when that party, acting reasonably, had determined that all other appropriate dispute resolution steps have not or will not be productive.

7.09 Good Faith and Reasonableness
The parties hereto covenant and agree each with the other to at all times be faithful, honest, and reasonable and conduct themselves in the utmost of good faith and reasonableness in order to further their mutual interest and the interest of the Clients.

7.10 Entire Agreement
This agreement and any schedules referred to herein constitute the entire agreement between the parties hereto.

7.11 Amendments
No modification or amendment to this Agreement may be made unless agreed to by the parties in writing.

IN WITNESS WHEREOF the parties hereto have duly executed this agreement under seal as of the day and year first written above.

SIGNED, SEALED & DELIVERED

Thomas Green ___   Ann Black ___

B
WORKSHEETS TO PROFILE THE PRACTICE

Whether you are a potential seller or a potential buyer, the better you understand your current client base and that of the other party, the better prepared you will be to negotiate a successful transaction.

In order to enable potential buyers to perform their due diligence and understand what the seller has to offer, the seller will need to disclose the details of their business. The better potential buyers understand their current client base, and how that compares to the seller's business, the clearer it will be whether or not the seller's practice is a good fit.

These worksheets can be used to profile either the seller's or the buyer's practice. Potential buyers may want to use them to help them assess the fit, but they are under no obligation to disclose the details of their current practice to the seller.

The following worksheets will help:

- sellers prepare answers for some of the questions a potential buyer will ask
- buyers identify the issues to review during the preliminary and final due diligence of a practice that is up for sale.

While these worksheets do not consider every item, they can help you focus on the profile of the business.

INCOME AND REVENUE DETAILS

REVENUES (AFTER THE PRODUCTION GRID)

	Current year	Previous year	Two years ago

Commission Income

Life insurance	_____	_____	_____
Mutual Funds	_____	_____	_____
Proprietary products	_____	_____	_____
Segregated funds	_____	_____	_____
Wrap/Managed portfolios	_____	_____	_____
Sub-total	_____	_____	_____

Recurring trailer/service/renewal income paid by product suppliers

Life insurance renewals	_____	_____	_____
Mutual Funds	_____	_____	_____
Proprietary products	_____	_____	_____
Segregated funds	_____	_____	_____
Wrap/Managed portfolios	_____	_____	_____
Sub-total	_____	_____	_____

Other revenues paid by product supplier

Other: _____	_____	_____	_____
Other: _____	_____	_____	_____
Sub-total	_____	_____	_____

Other Income

Interest income	_____	_____	_____
Other: _____	_____	_____	_____
Sub-total	_____	_____	_____

	Current year	Previous year	Two years ago

Fees paid by clients

Fee based on
size of portfolio _____   _____   _____

Fee-for-service income
under retainer _____   _____   _____

One-time financial
planning income _____   _____   _____

Fees from tax services _____   _____   _____

Other: _____   _____   _____   _____

Sub-total _____   _____   _____

**Total revenues
(after the grid)** _____   _____   _____

REVENUES (BEFORE THE PRODUCTION GRID)

Commission & Fees _____   _____   _____

Are gross revenues for the next calendar year expected to be:
❑ Same
❑ Less
❑ More

TO FURTHER ANALYZE THE INCOME EARNED:

Commissions

One-time _____   _____   _____

Recurring _____   _____   _____

Other: _____   _____   _____   _____

Average revenues

Per client _____   _____   _____

Per client family _____   _____   _____

TO ASSESS INCOME CONCENTRATION

List top 15 clients based on gross revenues over the last 12 months

Client	Commissions	Fees	Other	Total
1. _____	_____	_____	_____	_____
2. _____	_____	_____	_____	_____
3. _____	_____	_____	_____	_____
4. _____	_____	_____	_____	_____
5. _____	_____	_____	_____	_____
6. _____	_____	_____	_____	_____
7. _____	_____	_____	_____	_____
8. _____	_____	_____	_____	_____
9. _____	_____	_____	_____	_____
10. _____	_____	_____	_____	_____
11. _____	_____	_____	_____	_____
12. _____	_____	_____	_____	_____
13. _____	_____	_____	_____	_____
14. _____	_____	_____	_____	_____
15. _____	_____	_____	_____	_____

TO ASSESS SOURCES OF INCOME

Over the last 12 months, where has your new business come from?

	# of New Clients	Assets Gathered	Income Generated (net of grid)
Cold calls	_____	_____	_____
Client referrals	_____	_____	_____
COI Referrals (accountants, lawyers)	_____	_____	_____
Direct mail	_____	_____	_____
Inherited when an advisor left	_____	_____	_____
Newsletters	_____	_____	_____
Purchased client assets	_____	_____	_____
Referrals from friends	_____	_____	_____
Seminars	_____	_____	_____
Other: ____	_____	_____	_____

TO ASSESS ASSETS RELATED TO LEVERAGE

Value of client assets linked to borrowed money.

	Current year	Previous year	2 Years ago
Margin	_____	_____	_____
Home Equity	_____	_____	_____
Line of Credit	_____	_____	_____
Other: ____	_____	_____	_____

EXPENSES

	Current year	Previous year	2 years ago
Salaries and benefits			
Advisor salaries			
Staff salaries			
Payroll Costs (EI, CPP, etc.)			
Bonuses			
Benefits			
Other: _____			
Marketing			
Advertising			
Client events			
Entertainment			
Promotion			
Prospecting events			
Seminars			
Other: _____			
CE/PD			
Convention (incl. travel)			
External staff training			
On-line courses			
Seminars/workshops			
Other: _____			

	Current Year	Previous year	2 years ago
Office expenses			
Amortization			
Books/Journals			
Long distance costs			
Office insurance			
Office supplies			
Overhead insurance			
Postage and courier			
Printing costs			
Rent			
Subscriptions			
Utilities			
Other: _____			
Equipment			
Amortization			
Service/maintenance			
Computer leases			
Other leasing costs			
Phone/Wireless			
Service/maintenance			
Other: _____			
Software			
Internet service			
Licensing fees			
Software purchases			
Web hosting			
Other: _____			

	Current year	Previous year	2 years ago
Other			
Car insurance	_____	_____	_____
Car lease/payments	_____	_____	_____
Car service	_____	_____	_____
Depreciation	_____	_____	_____
Errors/omission insur.	_____	_____	_____
Fees paid to firm	_____	_____	_____
Fees paid to regulators	_____	_____	_____
Interest	_____	_____	_____
Parking fees	_____	_____	_____
Professional fees	_____	_____	_____
Professional liability	_____	_____	_____
Reimbursement re: client errors	_____	_____	_____
Travel	_____	_____	_____
Other: _____	_____	_____	_____
Total Expenses	_____	_____	_____

CLIENT ASSETS

VALUE OF INVESTMENT ASSETS MANAGED - BY YEAR

	Current year	Previous year	2 years ago
Investment Assets			
Canadian dollars	_____	_____	_____
U.S. dollars	_____	_____	_____
Other: _____	_____	_____	_____
Insurance face amount	_____	_____	_____

Number of investment clients _____

Number of investment client families _____

Total number of investment accounts _____

Average Investment Portfolio Size

Per client _____

Per client family _____

Number of insurance policyowners _____

Number of insurance client families _____

Total number of insurance policies _____

ASSESSING RATE OF ATTRITION/RETENTION

Clients who transferred their assets out in the last three years

	# of Clients	Value of Assets	Why?
Year_____	_____	_____	_____
Year_____	_____	_____	_____
Year_____	_____	_____	_____

LIST OF CLIENTS POTENTIALLY AT RISK

Names	Value of portfolio	Why?
_____	_____	_____
_____	_____	_____
_____	_____	_____
_____	_____	_____
_____	_____	_____
_____	_____	_____
_____	_____	_____
_____	_____	_____
_____	_____	_____

ASSETS MANAGED—BY ACCOUNT TYPE

	Number of accounts	$ assets held
RRSPs	_____	_____
Group RRSPs	_____	_____
Locked-in RRSPs	_____	_____
RRIFs	_____	_____
LIFs/LIRAs	_____	_____
RESPs	_____	_____
In-trust for accounts	_____	_____
Investment accounts	_____	_____
Group plans	_____	_____
IRAs	_____	_____
401(k)s	_____	_____
Trusts	_____	_____
Other: _____	_____	_____
Total	_____	_____

ASSETS MANAGED—BY PRODUCT TYPE

Show dollar value of the assets held as of the last day of _____, 20__

GICs/Term deposits

Maturing in less than one year	_____
Maturing in 1-3 years	_____
Maturing in more than 3 years	_____

Government or corporate bonds

Maturing in less than one year	_____
Maturing in 1-3 years	_____
Maturing in more than 3 years	_____

Mutual funds

	Load	DSC	No-load
Money market	_____	_____	_____
Fixed income	_____	_____	_____
Balanced	_____	_____	_____
Domestic equity	_____	_____	_____
International equity	_____	_____	_____
Other: _____	_____	_____	_____

Segregated funds

	Load	DSC	No-load
Money market	_____	_____	_____
Fixed income	_____	_____	_____
Balanced	_____	_____	_____
Domestic equity	_____	_____	_____
International equity	_____	_____	_____
Other: _____	_____	_____	_____

Other managed money

Wrap accounts	_____
Managed money	_____

Proprietary investments   _____

Discretionary accounts   _____

Stocks

Value   _____

Growth   _____

Speciality   _____

Penny   _____

Other

Real estate   _____

Private client services _____

Limited partnerships   _____

Banking services   _____

Loans/mortgages   _____

Trust services   _____

Other: _____ .   _____

Total Value of Assets Held _____

INVESTMENT ASSETS MANAGED—BY CLIENT PORTFOLIO SIZE

	# of clients	Value of accounts
< 100,000	_____	_____
100,000-249,999	_____	_____
250,000-499,999	_____	_____
500,000-749,999	_____	_____
750,000-999,999	_____	_____
1,000,000-2,499,999	_____	_____
2,500,000-4,999,999	_____	_____
5,000,000-9,999,999	_____	_____
10 million +	_____	_____
Totals	_____	_____

INSURANCE ASSETS—BY POLICY TYPE

	# of Policies	Value of insurance
Annuities		
Deferred	_____	_____
Variable	_____	_____

Individual life insurance

Term	_____	_____
Term-to-100	_____	_____
Whole Life	_____	_____
Universal Life	_____	_____
Disability	_____	_____
Critical illness	_____	_____
Other: _____	_____	_____

Group Life	# of Policies	Total premiums
Life insurance	_____	_____
Disability Insurance	_____	_____
Other: _____	_____	_____

Property and Casualty

Vehicle	_____	_____
Personal property	_____	_____
Commercial	_____	_____
Other: _____	_____	_____

New life insurance business placed

As of the last quarter	_____
One year earlier	_____
Two years earlier	_____
New business pending	_____

PROFILE OF CLIENTS

PROFILE OF INVESTMENT CLIENTS—BY AGE

Age	# of Clients	AUM	Insurance Needs Addressed?	
Under 35	_____	_____	❑ Yes	❑ No
35-44	_____	_____	❑ Yes	❑ No
45-54	_____	_____	❑ Yes	❑ No
55-69	_____	_____	❑ Yes	❑ No
70+	_____	_____	❑ Yes	❑ No

Average age   _____

PROFILE OF INVESTMENT CLIENTS—NUMBER OF YEARS AS CLIENT

	# of Clients	AUM
< 1 year	_____	_____
1-3 years	_____	_____
4-7 years	_____	_____
8-10 years	_____	_____
11+ years	_____	_____

PROFILE OF INVESTMENT CLIENTS—BY LIFECYCLE/OCCUPATION

	# of Clients	AUM
Assets held for minors	_____	_____
Baby Boomers	_____	_____
Business Owner/Entrepreneurs	_____	_____
Professionals	_____	_____
Retirees	_____	_____
Under 40	_____	_____
Widows/Widowers	_____	_____
Other: _____	_____	_____

PROFILE OF INSURANCE CLIENTS—BY AGE

Age	# of clients	Value of Insurance	Investment Needs Addressed?
Under 35	_____	_____	☐ Yes ☐ No
35-44	_____	_____	☐ Yes ☐ No
45-54	_____	_____	☐ Yes ☐ No
55-69	_____	_____	☐ Yes ☐ No
70+	_____	_____	☐ Yes ☐ No

Average age _____

PROFILE OF INSURANCE CLIENTS—YEARS INSURANCE IN FORCE

	# of Clients	Insurance face value
< 1 year	_____	_____
1-3 years	_____	_____
4-7 years	_____	_____
8-10 years	_____	_____
11-15 years	_____	_____
16-20 years	_____	_____
20+ years	_____	_____

PROFILE OF INSURANCE CLIENTS—BY LIFECYCLE/OCCUPATION

	# of Clients	AUM
Assets held for minors	_____	_____
Baby Boomers	_____	_____
Business Owner/Entrepreneurs	_____	_____
Professionals	_____	_____
Retirees	_____	_____
Under 40	_____	_____
Widows/Widowers	_____	_____
Other: _____	_____	_____

Approximate total net worth of clients (include all real estate, business and financial assets)

	# of Clients	Total Net Worth
< 100,000	_____	_____
100,000-249,999	_____	_____
250,000-499,999	_____	_____
500,000-749,999	_____	_____
750,000-999,999	_____	_____
1,000,000-2,499,999	_____	_____
2,500,000-4,999,999	_____	_____
5,000,000-9,999,999	_____	_____
10 million +	_____	_____

OTHER

Add any additional information relevant to the types of clients you serve.

_____

_____

_____

PROFILING THE ADVISOR AND THE PRACTICE

Been in practice since _____

What is the focus of the practice?
❏ Asset/Investment management
❏ Estate planning
❏ Financial planning
❏ Group RRSP/401(k)
❏ Pension assets
❏ Retirement planning
❏ Tax planning
❏ Tax preparation
❏ Other: _____

Form of ownership
❏ Commissioned employee
❏ Franchise
❏ Independent contractor
❏ Partnership
❏ Shareholder
❏ Sole proprietor
❏ Other: _____

Hours worked per week _____
Weeks worked per year _____

Compensation method (check all that apply)

❑ Commission

❑ Fee-for-service

❑ Recurring fees paid by client

❑ Recurring fees paid by product suppliers

❑ Other: _____

❑ Combination

Licenses held

Type	In which provinces and/or states are these licences held?
❑ Insurance	_____
❑ Labour sponsored funds	_____
❑ Mutual funds	_____
❑ Segregated funds	_____
❑ Stocks	_____
❑ Investment counselling	_____
❑ RIA	_____
❑ Other: _____	_____
❑ None	

Designations held

❑ None	❑ CA	❑ CFA	❑ CIM
❑ CPF	❑ FCSI	❑ PFP	❑ RFP
❑ Others: _____			

Memberships/Associations

❑ None	❑ CAIFA	❑ CAFP	❑ FPA
❑ IDA	❑ MFDA	❑ Other: _____	

Errors and Omission Insurance in force

❑   No ❑ Yes   Name of Carrier _____

Amount of Coverage _____

Deductible _____

Do you have a written

Business plan?   ❑ No ❑ Yes

Marketing plan?   ❑ No ❑ Yes

Staff

#	Licensed?	Years of service	Non-compete agreement
___Marketing assistant	❑ No ❑ Yes	_____ _____	❑ No ❑ Yes
___ Service assistant	❑ No ❑ Yes	_____ _____	❑ No ❑ Yes
___ Other _____	❑ No ❑ Yes	_____ _____	❑ No ❑ Yes
___ None			

Do you anticipate employees would be willing to work with the buyer?

❑ No ❑ Yes ❑ Don't know

Are other financial planners/advisors involved or on record?

❑ No ❑ Yes   If yes, are they   ❑ Formal partners

❑ Informal partners

❑ Insurance specialist

❑ Investment specialist

❑ Corporate consultant

❑ Other: _____

Number of investment companies dealt with _____

List of top 8 investment companies

% of your investment assets with them

1. _____   _____
2. _____   _____
3. _____   _____
4. _____   _____
5. _____   _____
6. _____   _____
7. _____   _____
8. _____   _____

Number of insurance companies dealt with _____

List of top 8 insurance companies

% of your insurance policies with them

1. _____   _____
2. _____   _____
3. _____   _____
4. _____   _____
5. _____   _____
6. _____   _____
7. _____   _____
8. _____   _____

Client management system

❑ ACT   ❑ Bill Good   ❑ CCB
❑ Maximizer   ❑ RPM   ❑ Winfund
❑ Other: _____

Back office

❑ Firm's   ❑ MRS   ❑ Laurentian Bank
❑ Other: _____

Financial Planning Software used

❑ FPS   ❑ Infomack   ❑ In sync

❑ Naviplan   ❑ PlanPlus   ❑ Profile

❑ RAM Wealth Creator   ❑ RRIFmetic   ❑ What If

❑ Other: _____

Do you prepare:

No   *Yes*

❑   ❑   Risk Tolerance Questionnaires/Profiles
                  If yes, for what percentage of clients? _____

❑   ❑   Written Investment Policy Statements
                  If yes, for what percentage of clients? _____

❑   ❑   Personalized Rates of Return
                  If yes, for what percentage of clients? _____

❑   ❑   Written Letters of Engagement or
                  Financial Planning Agreements
                  If yes, for what percentage of clients? _____

❑   ❑   Written Comprehensive Financial Plans
                  If yes, for what percentage of clients? _____

❑   ❑   Written Modular Financial Plans
                  If yes, for what percentage of clients? _____

SERVICE LEVELS

Some advisors differentiate among their platinum, gold, silver and bronze clients. Others by A, B, C and D clients. Describe the different service levels you provide clients.

Client service package   Clients qualify for this package if

1. _____   _____

2. _____   _____

3. _____   _____

4. _____   _____

5. _____   _____

Client service activities

(Indicate *M-monthly, Q-quarterly, S-semi-annually, A-annually, where appropriate.)

No	Yes						
❑	❑	New client package					
❑	❑	Phone contact with advisor	M	Q	S	A	N/A
❑	❑	Phone contact with assistant	M	Q	S	A	N/A
❑	❑	Face-to-face meeting	M	Q	S	A	N/A
❑	❑	Personalized mailings of interest	M	Q	S	A	N/A
❑	❑	Newsletter	M	Q	S	A	N/A
❑	❑	E-mail correspondence	M	Q	S	A	N/A
❑	❑	Written agenda for meetings					
❑	❑	Follow-up letter after meetings					
❑	❑	Written letter of engagement					
❑	❑	Financial plan updated	M	Q	S	A	N/A
❑	❑	Investment reviews	M	Q	S	A	N/A
❑	❑	Investment policy statement updated					
❑	❑	Client statements show personalized rate of return	M	Q	S	A	N/A
❑	❑	Consolidated client statements					
❑	❑	On-line account balances					
❑	❑	On-line research					
❑	❑	24-hour phone response					
❑	❑	Educational seminars	M	Q	S	A	N/A
❑	❑	Entertainment	M	Q	S	A	N/A

Describe the systems/processes you have in place for client retention

_____

_____

_____

OTHER ASSETS/LIABILITIES

OTHER ASSETS

Is it required that the buyer of the client assets also acquire the other assets of the business?

❑ No ❑ Yes ❑ Negotiable

	Description	Date purchased	Today's value
Real estate	_____	_____	_____

Office furniture

Chairs	_____	_____	_____
Desks	_____	_____	_____
Cadenzas	_____	_____	_____
Reception area	_____	_____	_____
Board room	_____	_____	_____
Filing cabinets	_____	_____	_____
Book shelves	_____	_____	_____
Other: _____	_____	_____	_____

Trademark(s)   _____

Name of the Company   _____

Office equipment

Phone system	_____	_____	_____
Fax machine	_____	_____	_____
Binding machine	_____	_____	_____
Shredder	_____	_____	_____

Computers   (attach list)

Describe the computer equipment that is also for sale, including year, make, model, serial number and features. If the equipment is on lease, include the details of the lease, including the amount and number of payments remaining, the buyout option, etc. Include desktops, laptops, printers, modems, network equipment, etc.

_____

_____

_____

Software (attach list)

Describe any software that you own where the license can be transferred. Include the name of the software, the version and year. Also indicate if the software is transferable. Include

	Description
Contact management	_____
Financial planning	_____
Investment management tools	_____
Prospecting and marketing	_____
Statements and reporting	_____
Other: _____	_____

DEBTS AND LIABILITIES

	Amount	Details
Debts	_____	_____
	_____	_____
Liabilities	_____	_____
	_____	_____

INTERESTED IN BUYING OR SELLING A BOOK OF BUSINESS?

CONFIDENTIAL REGISTRY

Are you looking to buy a book of business? Looking to sell your book of business? Or a part of your book?

List your interest with us on our confidential registry, where interested buyers and sellers can register for free by completing and faxing in our personal Buying or Selling An Advisory Practice Questionnaire (pdf found at www.headspringconsulting.com). Where there is a match, Headspring Consulting Inc. will make confidential introductions according to the instructions of both parties.

CONSULTING SERVICES FOR BUYERS AND SELLERS

Sandra Foster's consulting service for buying and selling a book of business involves, but is not limited, to the following:

- Workshops for advisors who are looking to buy/sell their practice that could be part of your professional development day.
- Consulting services for buyers who want assistance evaluating the potential of the business being considered.

- Consulting services for sellers who want to prepare their business for sale.
- Developing effective transition plans.
- Negotiating the terms of the agreement.
- Operating a blind pool for sellers who want to remain confidential as to their intentions for as long as possible.

Foster also assists corporations in developing internal policies for their advisors who are interested in buying or selling their books of business to assist with recruitment, advisor retention, asset retention and ease the transfer in the event of disability, death or retirement.

ABOUT HEADSPRING CONSULTING INC.

Founded by financial expert and national best-selling author Sandra Foster, Headspring Consulting Inc.'s mandate is to provide quality advice and expertise to the financial services industry and financial education to Canadians. We work with financial advisory firms, mutual fund dealers, brokerage houses, insurance companies, product manufacturers, as well as individual financial planners, advisors, brokers and insurance representatives. Our services include, but are not limited to:

PROFESSIONAL DEVELOPMENT

On a corporate or individual basis

- **Consulting: Strategic Advice & Research**, including the 2001 Financial Advice in Canada study, regarding change, emerging trends, acquiring a business, communications, reputation management, financial advice and financial planning, business planning, wealth management and more.
- **Keynote Presentations & Workshops** for conferences, corporate meetings and special events.
- **Policy & Procedures Manuals** to meet your MFDA requirements.

- **Written Materials & Tools** including books, articles and custom communications.

CONSUMER EDUCATION

Based on the national best-selling books by Sandra Foster
- **Client Appreciation/Prospecting Seminars** for firms and advisors.
- **Employee Benefit Programs** to prepare executives and employees for their financial futures. Programs include presentations, written materials and tools.
- **Books and Tools** based on Sandra Foster's books, and
- **Expertise** to the media.

Visit
www.headspringconsulting.com
www.whosmindingyourmoney.com

ABOUT
SANDRA FOSTER

Sandra Foster is a well-recognized expert and leading voice in the Canadian financial services community. Foster served as vice-president of a major financial advisory firm where she developed a successful financial advisory practice from 1993 to 1999, working with high-net-worth families, entrepreneurs and executives. Prior to selling her book of business in 1999, she spent over a year researching key issues in transactions involving financial advisory and planning firms in North America. Since then she has conducted leading-edge research on financial advice, developed and presented numerous keynote addresses and workshops, been invited to help firms develop internal policies for their planners, brokers and advisors, and helped advisors build their businesses and others to exit gracefully from their role as practising financial advisors. She has also worked with dentists and lawyers in their business planning.

Foster has published numerous articles in both consumer and industry media including *Advisor's Edge, MENZ, Costco Connections* and *Fifty-Plus* magazines, and has three best-selling books to her credit:
- *You Can't Take It With You: The Common-Sense Guide to Estate Planning for Canadians*

- *Make the Most of What You've Got: The Canadian Guide to Managing Retirement Income*
- *Who's Minding Your Money? Financial Intelligence for Canadian Investors*

She is frequently quoted and her comments have appeared in *The Globe and Mail, Canada AM, The National Post, Studio 2, The Toronto Star, CP24, Macleans, The Washington Post, CBC MoneyShow, MoneySense, ROBtv, IE:Money*, and more.

Foster holds the following designations: Certified Financial Planner (CFP), Registered Financial Planner (RFP), Certified Investment Manager (CIM), Certified Human Resources Professional (CHRP), Trust and Estate Practitioner (TEP), and Fellow, Canadian Securities Institute (FCSI).

Foster is currently a member of the Editorial Advisory Board for Advisor's Edge magazine, the Canadian Journal of Financial Planning and national committee of the Society of Trust & Estate Practitioners (STEP). She was also the recipient of the 1998 CAFP Multi-Media award. Foster holds a BA from the University of Toronto and is a graduate of the University of Toronto Executive Program. Prior to that, she ran a computer consulting firm.

Foster is located in Toronto, Canada.